ENGLISH
Idioms

Redewendungen,
Phrasal Verbs und
Anwendungsbeispiele

Compact Verlag

Bisher sind in dieser Reihe erschienen:

- English Idioms
- Englisch Wörterbuch
- Englisch Grammatik
- English Conversation
- Business English Wörterbuch
- Französisch Wörterbuch
- Französisch Grammatik
- Spanisch Wörterbuch
- Spanisch Grammatik
- Italienisch Wörterbuch
- Italienisch Grammatik
- Polnisch Wörterbuch
- Deutsch Rechtschreibung
- Deutsch Fremdwörter
- Deutsch Grammatik
- Deutsch Synonyme
- Mathematik
- Physik
- Chemie

Weitere Titel sind in Vorbereitung.

Chefredaktion: Dr. Angela Sendlinger
Redaktion: Helga Aichele
Produktion: Wolfram Friedrich
Umschlaggestaltung: Inga Koch

ISBN 978-3-8174-7778-4
7277781

Besuchen Sie uns im Internet: www.compactverlag.de

Vorwort

Eine Fremdsprache zu beherrschen, heißt auch, die Idiomatik der Sprache im Griff zu haben. Besonders im Englischen werden im täglichen Sprachgebrauch viele Redewendungen und Sprichwörter verwendet, die sich nicht einfach durch eine wörtliche Übersetzung oder das Nachschlagen in einem Wörterbuch erklären lassen.

Das richtige und sichere Verwenden der *Idioms* bedeutet, sich elegant und lebendig in einer Sprache auszudrücken. Doch dass dies nicht immer ein leichtes Unterfangen ist, macht gerade die englische Idiomatik deutlich, die ihre ganz spezifischen, spracheigentümlichen Tücken birgt. Die so genannten *Phrasal Verbs*, eine Kombination aus Verb und Präposition oder Adverb, haben oft stark abweichende Bedeutungen. Auch werden in der englischen Idiomatik z. T. ganz andere Bilder benutzt als wir sie aus dem Deutschen kennen.

Das vorliegende Buch ist speziell dafür konzipiert, zu einem zuverlässigen und gewandten Umgang mit der englischen Idiomatik zu führen.
Die häufigsten englischen idiomatischen Wendungen werden auf lernerfreundliche Art dem Benutzer nahegebracht: alphabetische Anordnung, Kennzeichnung der Stilebene, griffige Übersetzungen, erklärende Umschreibungen und leicht verständliche Beispielsätze dienen dazu, sich den Stoff Schritt für Schritt anzueignen und leichter einzuprägen. Ein Register am Ende des Buches ermöglicht das gezielte und schnelle Auffinden bestimmter englischer *Idioms* über das entsprechende deutsche Stichwort.

„English Idioms" ist der ideale Begleiter für alle, die ein einwandfreies und flüssiges idiomatisches Englisch sprechen möchten.

Abkürzungen

Am.	amerikanisch
Brit.	britisch
jdm.	jemandem
jdn.	jemanden
jds.	jemandes
jmd.	jemand
o.s.	oneself
s.b.	somebody
Sl.	Slang
s.o.	someone
s.th.	something

A

able:

~ to breathe (easily/ freely) again *Now that the crisis is over, we are all able to breathe easily again.*	aufatmen können
~ to do something blindfold(ed)/~ to do something standing on one's head *Brian is an amazing driver – he is able to win the race blindfolded.*	etwas mit links erledigen
~ to take a joke	einen Spaß verstehen (können)
~ to take something	etwas aushalten können

about:

be ~ eight years old	ungefähr acht Jahre alt sein
be ~ to do s.th.	drauf und dran sein, etwas zu tun
up and ~	wieder auf den Beinen
~ time *It is about time John brought back tho car!*	höchste Zeit
What ~ ... ?	Was ist mit ...?

above:

~ all	vor allem
~ board	offen, ehrlich
~ suspicion	über jeden Verdacht erhaben
~ one's station	das Benehmen entspricht nicht der sozialen Position
get ~ oneself *Don't get above yourself, you are no better than the rest of us.*	eingebildet sein, sich überschätzen

~ par	über dem Durchschnitt
not to be ~ doing s.th.	sich nicht zu fein sein, etwas zu tun
Absence makes the heart grow fonder. (Sprichw.)	Die Liebe wächst mit der Entfernung.
accent:	
to have an ~ you could cut with a knife	einen ausgeprägten Akzent haben
accident:	
~s will happen.	Auf so etwas muss man immer gefasst sein.
by ~	zufällig
meet with an ~	verunglücken
accord:	
of one's own ~	aus eigenem Antrieb, von selbst, von sich aus
with one ~	einstimmig
~ing to all accounts	alle behaupten; laut Berichten/Aussagen
~ing to s.o. or s.th.	laut ...
~ing to one's lights	im Rahmen seiner Möglichkeiten
account	
~ for	erklären
Did they account for the delay?	
of no ~	bedeutungslos
on ~ of	auf Grund
She left her husband on account of his infidelity.	
on no ~ of	keineswegs
a few little aches and pains	ein paar Wehwehchen
acid test	Feuerprobe
across the board	für jeden gleich
The government decided to raise the taxes across the board.	

act:

~ the giddy goat	sich wie ein Trottel benehmen
~ of God	höhere Gewalt
~ upon/on	auf Grund von etwas handeln
We have told them what to do – now it's up to them to act on our advice.	
~ up	Theater machen, sich aufspielen, sich daneben benehmen
get in on the ~	auf einen fahrenden Zug aufspringen
get one's ~ together	sich zusammenreißen
be in the ~ of	gerade dabei sein, etwas zu tun
He was caught in the act of stealing the car.	
~ one's age	sich seinem Alter gemäß verhalten, nicht albern sein
Stop being so childish, Susan. Act your age!	

action:

~s speak louder than words.	Taten zählen mehr als Worte.
to get a piece of the ~	ein Stück vom Kuchen abbekommen
~ stations	sich bereit machen
Once it had become clear that the tornado was coming, it was action stations all around.	

active service	(noch) im Dienst
in actual fact	tatsächlich
add up to s.th.	1. eine mathematische Summe bilden, 2. bedeuten
1. The shopping adds up to almost a hundred pounds. *2. I don't see what all this adds up to. What do you mean?*	
to come adrift	verloren gehen

advantage:	
to have the ~ of	den Vorteil haben
He had the advantage of a first-class education.	
to take ~ of	1. jdn. ausnutzen, 2. eine Gelegenheit nutzen
1. The car dealer took advantage of his customer's gullibility. *2. I look advantage of the fine weather to play tennis.*	
after:	
~ a fashion	mehr oder weniger
~ all	schließlich, letztendlich, doch
The party did not seem very enjoyable at the beginning but in the end, everybody had a good time after all.	
~ all is said and done	schließlich, unterm Strich
After all was said and done the holiday was a success.	
~ hours	nach Büro- oder Ladenschluss
He would often remain in the office after hours to complete his work.	
be ~ s.o./s.th	jdm./etwas hinterherjagen
The bankrobber knew the police would be after him.	
again:	
~ and ~	immer wieder
as much ~	noch einmal so viel
now and ~	ab und zu
there ~	andererseits
time and ~	immer wieder
against:	
~ s.o.'s better judgement	wider besseres Wissen
~ the clock	im Wettlauf mit der Zeit
~ the grain	gegen den Strich
~ (the/all) odds	gegen starken Widerstand, entgegen aller Erwartungen
as ~ him	im Vergleich zu ihm

age:

act one's ~	nicht albern sein, sich seinem Alter gemäß benehmen
at an advanced ~	im hohen Alter
be of ~	volljährig sein
come of ~	volljährig werden
for ~s	seit langer Zeit

agree:

~ with s.o.	die Meinung von jdm. teilen
not ~ with s.o.	jdm. nicht bekommen, krank machen

Travelling by boat does not agree with me, it always makes me feel sick.

ahead:

~ of time	vorher, vor der angekündigten Zeit, früher

If you get there ahead of time you'll just have to wait.

get ~	Karriere machen

It takes a lot of ambition if you really want to get ahead.

air:

~ one's knowledge	sein Wissen unter Beweis stellen
~ one's views	seine Meinung verkünden
in the ~	1. ungewiss, 2. in der Luft liegen

1. We go to Paris tomorrow, but after that our plans are in the air.
2. There are rumours in the air of a strike at the factory.

clear the ~	die Situation klären
give o.s. ~s	sich zieren, vornehm tun
~s and graces	Allüren

Aladdin's cave	eine Schatzkammer

alive:

~ and kicking	lebendig, aktiv

It's good to see uncle Bob is still alive and kicking.

~ to s.th.	sich einer Sache bewusst sein
~ with	wimmeln von, voll sein von
The river was alive with fish.	

all:

~ agog	in freudiger Erwartung
Everybody was all agog for the play to start.	
~ alone	ganz allein
~ along	die ganze Zeit
~ being well	wenn sonst nichts schief geht
All being well, we should catch the plane.	
~ the best	Viel Glück!
~ right	in Ordnung
~ the same	dennoch, trotzdem
for ~ I care	meinetwegen
for ~ I know	so viel ich weiß, schon möglich
not at ~	überhaupt nicht
~ but	beinahe, fast
to be ~ ears	ganz Ohr sein
on ~ fours	auf allen vieren
~ in	1. fertig, erschöpft, 2. alles zusammen
1. They're all in after their marathon run. *2. The holiday will cost $ 200 all in.*	
~ in a day's work	gehört zu den Aufgaben, typisch
~ in good time	alles zu seiner Zeit
~ in all	alles in allem
~ in one piece	sicher, unversehrt, heil
~ my eye (and Betty Martin) (Am./Sl.)	Quatsch/vollkommener Unsinn
That's all my eye and Betty Martin. Don't believe a word of it.	
~ one	unwichtig, egal
It's all one to me whether you go or stay.	
~ out	mit Volldampf
The workers are going all out to finish the job by the end of the week.	

~ over	1. überall, 2. vorbei, 3. typisch für
1. There were celebrations all over town.	
2. They did not leave until the excitement was all over.	
3. John handed in his essay late, but that's John all over.	
~ the same	1. gleich, 2. trotzdem
1. It's all the same to me.	
2. All the same, I think you're wrong.	
~ set	absolut bereit
All set? Then we can leave.	
~ and sundry	alle, Hinz und Kunz
for ~ that	trotzdem
to be ~ things to ~ men	es allen Leuten recht machen wollen
when ~'s said and done	unterm Strich, letzten Endes
~ the rage	der letzte Schrei
It seems to be all the rage for young girls to dye their hair green.	
not ~ there (Sl.)	nicht ganz bei Trost
~ thumbs	zwei linke Hände, ungeschickt
~'s well that ends well. (Sprichw.)	Ende gut, alles gut!
~ year round	das ganze Jahr über/hindurch

allow:

~ for s.o. or s.th.	in Betracht ziehen, berücksichtigen
Did you allow for any delays?	
~ of no argument	keinen Einwand zulassen, keinen Widerspruch dulden
make allowance(s)	Nachsicht üben wegen, berücksichtigen
We must make allowance(s) for her inexperience.	

along:

~ with	zusammen mit, in Gesellschaft von
be ~ in a minute	gleich kommen
I'll be along in a minute.	
~ the lines of	in der Art von
go ~ with (Sl.)	zustimmen, mitmachen

an eye for an eye, a tooth for a tooth	Auge um Auge, Zahn um Zahn
to be an also-ran	unter „ferner liefen“ rangieren
to take s.th. amiss	etwas übel nehmen
and:	
~ **all that**	und so weiter
~ **a half**	mehr als üblich
~ **howl!** (Sl.)	und ob! aber wie!
He is a great driver! – And howl! He can beat anybody!	
~ **no mistake**	aber sicher
~ **one knows it**	man weiß
~ **the like**	und Ähnliches
~ **what not** (Sl.)	und so weiter und so fort
angel:	
~ **of death**	Todesengel
~ **of light**	Lichtengel
~ **of mercy**	rettender Engel
another cup of tea	eine ganz andere Sache
answer:	
~ **back**	frech werden, widersprechen
My mother always scolded me if I answered back.	
~ **for**	die Verantwortung übernehmen
~ **a purpose**	geeignet sein, einen Zweck erfüllen
~ **the call of duty**	seine Pflicht tun, eine Pflicht erfüllen
~ **to s.o.**	sich jemandem gegenüber rechtfertigen
~ **(to)**	1. übereinstimmen, entsprechen, 2. hören auf
1. A man answering (to) that description was seen leaving the bank. 2. He answers to the name of John Doe.	

any:

~ day	wann immer möglich
to not have ~ of it	nichts davon wissen wollen
~ old (Sl.)	jeder x-beliebige
~ minute now	jeden Moment

The film will start any minute now.

appearances:

to all ~	offensichtlich, anscheinend
keep up ~	den Schein wahren
~ are deceptive. (Sprichw.)	Der Schein trügt.

apple:

be the ~ of s.o.'s eye	jdm. besonders wert/ lieb sein

His baby daughter is the apple of his eye.

an ~ for the teacher (Sl.)	ein Versuch, sich beliebt zu machen
the ~ of discord	Zankapfel

argue the toss	sich mit einer Streitfrage auseinandersetzen

arm[1]:

~ in ~	Arm in Arm
keep s.b. at ~'s length	jdn. auf Distanz halten
within ~'s reach	in Reichweite

arm[2]:

~ o.s. against	sich gegen etwas wappnen
~ o.s. with s.th.	sich mit etwas bewaffnen
armed to the teeth (Sl.)	bis an die Zähne bewaffnet

around the clock	rund um die Uhr

as:

~ a duck takes to water	ohne Schwierigkeiten, natürlich

He took to playing the trumpet just as a duck takes to water.

~ for you	was dich betrifft

~ it were	sozusagen
~ yet	bis jetzt
I thought ~ much	Das hab' ich mir gedacht.
~ the case stands	wie die Dinge stehen
~ a rule	in der Regel
~ a last resort	als letzter Ausweg
My father was a peaceful man and only used beating as a last resort.	
~ a matter of course	selbstverständlich, an der Tagesordnung
You are expected to make your own bed as a matter of course.	
~ a matter of fact	im Übrigen
As a matter of fact, I saw him yesterday.	
~ and when	wann und wie
~ bad ~ ever	genau so schlimm wie eh und je
~ blind ~ a bat	stockblind
I'm getting as blind as a bat, I must get some spectacles.	
~ bold ~ brass	unverschämt
~ busy ~ a bee	eifrig, bienenfleißig
The children were as busy as bees, playing in the sand.	
~ clear ~ mud (Sl.)	sehr unverständlich
I'm afraid I can't see the point at all, your argument is as clear as mud.	
~ cool ~ a cucumber	die Ruhe selbst
She never loses her temper, she's as cool as a cucumber.	
~ dead ~ a dodo (Sl.)	mausetot
~ easy ~ falling off a log (Sl.)	sehr einfach, kinderleicht
~ easy ~ pie (Sl.)	babyleicht
~ far ~ I'm concerned	was mich betrifft
~ fit ~ a fiddle (Sl.)	kerngesund
The doctor told me I'm as fit as a fiddle.	
~ good ~ done	beinahe fertig/erledigt
~ good ~ gold (Sl.)	sehr brav
The baby was as good as gold.	
~ happy ~ a lark	quietschfidel

~ hard ~ nails	knallhart, steinhart
~ light ~ a feather	federleicht
~ mad ~ a March hare	total verrückt
~ mad ~ hell (Sl.)	wütend
~ of old	nach alter Sitte
~ plain ~ the nose on one's face (Sl.)	ganz offensichtlich
~ plain ~ day	sonnenklar
~ quick ~ a wink	blitzschnell
~ quick ~ greased lightning (Sl.)	wie ein geölter Blitz
~ regular ~ clockwork	präzise wie ein Uhrwerk
~ right ~ rain	in guter Verfassung
~ sick ~ a dog	hundeelend, speiübel
~ smart ~ a fox	sehr schlau, ausgefuchst
~ snug ~ a bug in a rug (Sl.) *The mother tucked her daughter up in bed and said: "There you are, as snug as a bug in a rug".*	warm, geborgen, sicher
~ sparks fly upward	mit absoluter Sicherheit
~ sure as ten dimes buy a dollar (Am.)	sicherlich
~ thick ~ thieves	unzertrennlich, wie Pech und Schwefel
~ thick ~ two short planks	dumm wie Bohnenstroh
~ to the manner born *She rides a horse as to the manner born.*	für etwas wie geschaffen sein
~ tough ~ old boots	zäh wie Leder
~ well ~ the next man	genau so gut wie jeder andere
~ white ~ snow	schneeweiß
~ wise ~ an owl	sehr weise

ask:

~ for the moon	das Unmögliche verlangen, nach den Sternen greifen
~ for trouble	Schwierigkeiten heraufbeschwören
~ me another!	Frag mich etwas Leichteres!
It's yours for the ~ing!	Du brauchst es nur zu sagen!

to look askance at s.o. or s.th.	misstrauisch betrachten, schief ansehen

at:

~ all	überhaupt

~ all costs	um jeden Preis
~ all times	ständig, immer
I have said it again and again, you have to tell me the truth at all times.	
~ any rate	auf jeden Fall
~ death's door	dem Tode nah
~ every turn	überall (wo man hinschaut)
The playful kitten gets under my feet at every turn.	
~ first	am Anfang, zuerst
~ hand	griffbereit
be ~ it again (Sl.)	schon wieder dabei sein, etwas zu tun
be ~ s.th. (Sl.)	etwas anstellen
~ length	ausführlich
~ some length	ziemlich lange
be ~ loggerheads	im Streit sein, sich in den Haaren liegen
The two brothers were always at loggerheads, they could never agree.	
~ long last	endlich
~ a loose end	rastlos, ziellos, unruhig, ohne Arbeit
John was at a loose end and was glad to join me for an evening in the cinema.	
(all) ~ sea	durcheinander, im Dunkeln tappen
~ odds with s.o.	uneins, im Streit
Don't pay attention to him, he's at odds with everyone today.	
~ one fell swoop	auf einen Schlag, auf einmal
~ one's wits' end	mit seiner Weisheit am Ende
I'm at my wits' end. What shall I do?	
~ short notice	kurzfristig
It is not easy to get an appointment with the dentist at short notice.	
~ the crack of dawn	bei Tagesanbruch, sehr früh
It's no fun, getting up to go to work at the crack of dawn.	

~ cross purposes	mit unterschiedlichen Zielen
~ the double	im Nu, im Eilschritt
~ the drop of a hat	im Nu, beim geringsten Anlass
Any elected official will defend the programme at the drop of a hat.	
~ the eleventh hour	fünf vor zwölf
~ the end of one's tether	fix und fertig
Stop getting on your mum's nerves, Alistair. Can't you see she's at the end of her tether.	
~ will	nach Belieben
no strings attached	konditionslos, ohne Nachteile
We received permission to use the old building with no strings attached.	
avenge:	
~ o.s. on s.b. for s.th.	sich für etwas an jdm. rächen
leave no avenue unexplored	alle Möglichkeiten ausschöpfen, alle möglichen Informationen einholen
to avoid s.o. like the plague	jdn. meiden wie die Pest
away:	
~ with that!	Weg damit!
right ~	jetzt gleich, sofort
to have it ~ with s.o. (Sl.)	eine Nummer schieben
an awful lot	sehr viel

B

baby:	
a ~ in arms	Säugling; schwach
a ~ in the woods (Am.)	Naivling
to be left holding the ~	die Verantwortung für etwas aufgebürdet bekommen; etwas allein ausbaden müssen
back:	
~ and forth	hin und her
bend over ~wards	sich übergroße Mühe geben
~ down	seine Meinung aufgeben
a ~ number	eine alte Ausgabe (einer Zeitung o. ä.)
~ off (Sl.)	in Ruhe lassen
~-seat driver	Besserwisser (der die Folgen nicht zu tragen braucht)
get off s.o.'s ~	jdn. in Ruhe lassen
to get s.o.'s ~ up	jdn. reizen, jdn. aus dem Häuschen bringen
~ s.o. or s.th. up	bestätigen
~stairs	geheim, nicht offiziell
You should not listen to backstairs gossip.	
go ~ upon one's word	sein Wort brechen
go ~ on s.o.	jdn. im Stich lassen
hang ~	zurück bleiben, sich im Hintergrund halten
with one's ~ to the wall	mit dem Rücken zur Wand
to put one's back into s.th.	sich in etwas reinknien
bad:	
~ blood	Feindschaft, böses Blut
Be careful what you do, there has been bad blood between them for a long time.	
~ form	schlechter Stil, unhöflich
I cannot believe he borrowed your car without telling you – that's terribly bad form.	

a ~ lot	bösartig, unzuverlässig
want s.th. ~ly	etwas unbedingt haben wollen
to be in a ~ way	in einer schwierigen Lage sein

bag:

in the ~	unter Dach und Fach
~ and baggage	mit Kind und Kegel
a ~ of nerves	ein Nervenbündel
a ~ of bones	spindeldürr, Haut und Knochen
~s of (Sl.)	reichlich
the whole ~ of tricks	alle möglichen Tricks

a baker's dozen	dreizehn (von der alten Sitte, einem Kunden, der zwölf Dinge in einer Bäckerei kaufte, ein Stück extra zu geben)

balance:

to hold the ~	das Zünglein an der Waage bilden
on ~	alles in allem
strike the ~	Bilanz ziehen

ball:

be on the ~	auf Draht sein
set the ~ rolling	den Stein ins Rollen bringen
have a ~	einen Mordsspaß haben
The ~'s in your court.	Jetzt sind Sie dran!

The balloon went up.	Die Bombe platzte.

bang:

~ in the middle	mittendrin, genau in der Mitte
~ one's head against a brick wall	mit dem Kopf gegen die Wand rennen
to go off with a ~	großartig funktionieren

bare:

~ one's heart	sein Herz ausschütten
~ one's teeth	die Zähne zeigen/fletschen
the ~ bones of s.th.	die Grundzüge von etwas

bargain:

~ counter	Wühltisch im Kaufhaus

~ing counter (Brit.) — Trumpfkarte bei Verhandlungen
~ for — rechnen mit
We didn't bargain for so many people coming to the party.
to be a ~ — ein Schnäppchen sein
to drive a hard ~ — zäh verhandeln
into the ~ — hinzu, obendrein
make the best of a bad ~ — das Beste draus machen
strike a ~ — einen Kompromiss schließen

bark:
His ~ is worse than his bite. — Bellende Hunde beißen nicht.
~ up the wrong tree — auf dem Holzweg sein

bat:
not to ~ an eyelid — nicht mit der Wimper zucken
like a ~ out of hell (Brit./Sl.) — wie ein geölter Blitz
He was so frightened he ran out of the house like a bat out of hell.
have ~s in the belfry (Sl.) — einen Vogel haben
off one's own ~ — auf eigene Faust, aus eigener Initiative, von sich aus

a bawling match (Sl.) — eine lautstarke Auseinandersetzung

be:
the ~-all and end-all — das A und O
for the time ~ing — zunächst, im Moment
~ a must (Sl.) — etwas, das man tun muss; es gehört dazu
It's a must that you visit Buckingham Palace when you're in London.
~ all ears — ganz Ohr sein
Do tell me your story. I'm all ears!
~ bushed (Am./Sl.) — erschöpft sein
~ poles apart — da liegen Welten dazwischen
~ in a blue funk (Sl.) — in wilder Panik sein
He was in a blue funk about having lost the documents.
~ on one's beam-end(s) — pleite sein
~ beside oneself with joy — vor Freude ganz aus dem Häuschen sein

~ that as it may	wie dem auch sei
~ the spitting image of s.o.	jdm. wie aus dem Gesicht geschnitten sein
He is the spitting image of his brother, it is hard to tell them apart.	

beans:

to be full of ~	voller Tatendrang sein
to spill the ~	ausplaudern, verraten

bear[1]:

~ fruit	Früchte tragen
~ up	durchhalten, standhalten
s.th. ~s watching	etwas muss im Auge behalten werden
Our situation is critical and will bear watching.	
~ in mind	etwas berücksichtigen
Bear what I have said in mind when you go for the interview.	
not to ~ close inspection	einer genaueren Untersuchung nicht standhalten können
a cross to ~	eine Last zu tragen

bear[2]:

like a ~ with a sore head	schlechte Laune, bärbeißig
~ garden	eine Räuberhöhle

beat:

~ about the bush	um den heißen Brei herum reden
Stop beating about the bush and come to the point.	
~ it (Am./Sl.)	abhauen, verschwinden
Mary turned up as well, but we told her to beat it.	
~ a retreat	den Rückzug antreten
We wanted to drive home despite the storm, but after a few minutes, we beat a hasty retreat to our hosts' house.	
~ s.o. down	herunterhandeln
~ the band	alle übertreffen oder überraschen

~ one's brains out	sich den Kopf zerbrechen
~ one's breast	öffentlich Reue zeigen
beauty:	
~ is in the eye of the beholder.	Schönheit liegt im Auge des Betrachters.
~ sleep	Schönheitsschlaf
becoming to s.o.	jdm. gut stehen
You should always wear that dress, it is very becoming to you.	
a bee in one's bonnet	eine fixe Idee, einen Tick haben
He has a bee in his bonnet about changing the world.	
before:	
~ long	bald, binnen kurzem
~ you can say knife	plötzlich, blitzschnell
~ you know it	bevor man sich versieht
carry all ~ one	sehr erfolgreich sein
beg:	
Beggar's can't be choosers.	In der Not frisst der Teufel Fliegen.
I shall take whatever job is offered, beggars can't be choosers.	
~ the question	eine Fage aufwerfen
~ to differ	anderer Meinung sein
beginner's luck	Anfängerglück
behave like a bull in a china shop	sich wie ein Elefant im Porzellanladen benehmen
behind:	
~ closed doors	hinter verschlossenen Türen
~ one's back	hinter jds. Rücken
~ the scenes	hinter den Kulissen
saved by the bell	in letzter Sekunde gerettet

have under one's belt	in der Tasche haben
bend:	
~ over backwards to do s.th.	sich übermäßig anstrengen, etwas zu tun
He is bending over backwards to get the task done.	
be round the ~	nicht alle Tassen im Schrank haben, verrückt sein
He is completely round the bend.	
the benefit of the doubt	im Zweifel für den Angeklagten
best:	
at the ~ of times	bestenfalls
~ bib and tucker (Sl.)	die feinste Kleidung, die man besitzt, Festkleidung
We had to go and see the boss, so I put on my best bib and tucker for the occasion.	
be all for the ~	zum Besten von jdm. sein
in the ~ of all possible worlds	unter perfekten Bedingungen
the ~ of British luck	(meist iron.) viel Glück dabei!
the ~ that money can buy	das Feinste vom Feinen
get the ~ of s.th.	am besten wegkommen
to the ~ of my knowledge	nach bestem Wissen
put the ~ foot forward	so schnell wie möglich gehen
bet one's bottom dollar	absolut sicher sein, alles darauf setzen
I'll bet my bottom dollar he is going to be late again!	
better:	
~ late than never	besser spät als nie
to think ~ of s.th.	es sich anders überlegen
to go one ~ than s.o.	jdn. übertreffen, eins draufsetzen
between:	
in ~	mittendrin, dazwischen
~ ourselves	unter uns
read ~ the lines	zwischen den Zeilen lesen

~ the devil and the deep blue sea (Sl.) — zwischen Hölle und Fegefeuer, in der Klemme
He couldn't make up his mind as to what to decide. He was obviously between the devil and the deep blue sea.
~ you, me and the gate-post (Brit/Sl.) — unter uns gesagt
Between you, me and the gate-post, their marriage is not going well.

beyond:
the back of ~ (Sl.) — wo sich Fuchs und Hase gute Nacht sagen
No wonder house prices are cheap in this area, it is the back of beyond, nobody would want to live here.
That's ~ me. — Das ist mir zu hoch.
live ~ one's means — über seine Verhältnisse leben
If we continue to live beyond our means we'll never get rich.
~ (all) bearing — unerträglich
~ all measure — über die Maßen
~ belief — unvorstellbar

bid somebody good-bye — sich von jdm. verabschieden

bide one's time — geduldig auf etwas warten

big:
the ~ battalions — die Mächtigen (mit negativem Anklang)
a ~ bug (Sl.) — jmd. Bedeutsames
a ~ cheese (Sl.) — hohes Tier
a ~ hit — großer Erfolg, großer Renner
So far, he had not earned a lot of money, but his new play was a big hit.
the ~ stick — überlegene Gewalt
to get too ~ for one's boots — größenwahnsinnig werden
the bigger the better — je mehr, desto besser

bill and coo	miteinander turteln
bind s.b. hand and foot	jdm. Freiheiten nehmen
bird:	
a ~ of passage	Wandervogel
the ~ has flown	der Vogel ist ausgeflogen
The early ~ catches the worm. (Sprichw.)	Morgenstund' hat Gold im Mund.
A ~ in the hand is worth two in the bush. (Sprichw.)	Ein Spatz in der Hand ist besser als eine Taube auf dem Dach.
~ s of a feather flock together. (Sprichw.)	Gleich und Gleich gesellt sich gern.
kill two ~s with one stone (Sl.)	zwei Fliegen mit einer Klappe schlagen
When you go to the chemist's for your prescription, you could bring me my medicine, that would be killing two birds with one stone.	
the ~s and the bees	die Bienchen und Blümchen
in one's birthday suit	nackt, im Adams-/Evakostüm
bit:	
~ by ~	Stück für Stück, nach und nach
a ~ much	ein starkes Stück
His request of both more pay and more days off work was a bit much.	
a ~ of all right (Sl., altmodisch)	große Klasse
a ~ thick	übertrieben; begriffsstutzig
bitch:	
~ about s.th.	über etwas lästern
a ~ of a day (Am.)	ein mieser Tag
bite:	
~ back a remark	sich eine Bemerkung verkneifen
~ off more than one can chew	sich zu viel zumuten
~ the dust	ins Gras beißen; scheitern
~ the hand that feeds you	den Ast absägen, auf dem man sitzt

bits and bobs	verschiedener Kleinkram
bitten:	
Once ~, twice shy.	Ein gebranntes Kind scheut das Feuer.
What's ~ him?	Was ist mit ihm los?
a bitter pill	schwer zu akzeptieren, eine bittere Pille
black:	
~ and blue	grün und blau (geschlagen)
be in s.b.'s ~ books	bei jdm. schlecht angeschrieben sein
a ~ day for s.b.	ein schlechter Tag für jdn.
a ~ look	ein finsterer Blick
a ~ mood	schlechte Laune
~ out	umkippen, das Bewusstsein verlieren
~ sheep of the family	das schwarze Schaf der Familie
in ~ and white	schwarz auf weiß
blacken:	
~ s.b.'s name	jdn. anschwärzen
~ the picture	etwas schlimmer machen, als es ist
blame the other fellow	Verantwortung für etwas weiterschieben
Whenever something went wrong, he blamed the other fellow.	
a wet blanket	ein Spielverderber
at full blast	auf Hochtouren
blaze a trail	den Weg bahnen, Pionierarbeit leisten
bleed s.b. white	jdn. (finanziell) ausnehmen
blind:	
a ~ alley	eine Sackgasse

~ drunk volltrunken
turn a ~ eye ein Auge zudrücken
a ~ fury rasende Wut
the ~ leading the ~ eine Situation, in der unfähige Leute andere unfähige Leute anweisen, etwas zu tun; ein Blinder führt einen Blinden
The attempted reorganisation is a classic case of the blind leading the blind, as nobody understands anything.
to have a ~ spot einen Schwachpunkt haben
~ to the world volltrunken

blink:
~ the fact eine Tatsache ignorieren
in the ~ of an eye urplötzlich, blitzschnell

blood:
~ is thicker than water. Blut ist dicker als Wasser.
He may be a thief but he is also my son, and I must help him. Blood is thicker than water.
bad ~ böses Blut
There has been bad blood between Zoe and her sister for ages.
blue ~ blaublütig, adlig
in cold ~ kaltblütig
The judge said the murderer had acted in cold blood, and therefore deserved the hardest punishment provided for by law.
squeeze ~ out of a stone jdm. etwas aus der Nase ziehen; verlorene Liebesmüh
Trying to get a straight answer out of him is like trying to squeeze blood out of a stone.
~ and gut gewalttätige Szenen in Film oder Theater

blot one's copy book (Brit.) sich unmöglich machen, seinen (guten) Ruf ruinieren

blow:	
~ the gaff (Sl.)	nicht dichthalten
~ hot and cold	sein Fähnchen nach dem Wind drehen
~ one's top (Sl.)	vor Wut explodieren; vor Wut in die Luft gehen
If you irritate him much more he'll blow his top.	
~ off steam	Dampf ablassen
Jack was so angry after the meeting, he just had to blow off steam.	
have a ~-out	sich vollfressen
~ up	die Beherrschung verlieren
~ s.th.	etwas verpatzen
~ s.th. sky-high	etwas vollständig zerstören, ein Argument total widerlegen
~ s.o. up (Sl.)	anschnauzen
~ the lid off s.th.	etwas verraten/aufdecken
The boys were angry with David for blowing the lid off their plans to run away from home.	
~ one's own trumpet	sich selber loben, angeben
She is not a modest person at all, she's always blowing her own trumpet.	
~ over	vorübergehen, aufhören
We often have a row, but they soon blow over.	
tell s.th. ~ by ~	in allen Einzelheiten erzählen/berichten
to get on the blower	sich an die Strippe hängen
blue:	
a ~ movie	ein Pornofilm
feel ~	deprimiert sein, Trübsal blasen
the ~-eyed boy	jds. Liebling, Goldjunge
a ~ fit	sich sehr über etwas ärgern
~ murder	Zeter und Mordio
There'll be blue murder when she hears of this.	
like a bolt from the ~	wie ein Blitz aus heiterem Himmel

His news came as a complete surprise, like a bolt from the blue.

once in a ~ moon	äußerst selten, alle Jubeljahre einmal

I have an aunt in Canada whom I see once in a blue moon.

blunder:

to ~ into s.th.	in etw. hineingeraten
to commit a ~	einen Fehler machen

boat:

be in the same ~	im selben Boot sitzen
have an oar in everyone's ~	überall seine Finger im Spiel haben
push the ~ out	keine Mühen (oder Kosten) scheuen

body:

a ~ blow	ein herber Rückschlag
~ and soul	ganz und gar

the bogey man	der schwarze Mann

to boil down to ...	darauf hinauslaufen, dass ...

What it all boils down to is that he is going to leave her.

bold:

as ~ as brass	unverschämt, frech wie Oskar
a ~ front	vorgetäuschter Mut oder gute Stimmung

bolt:

~ s.th. down	etwas herunterschlingen
a ~ from the blue	ein Blitz aus heiterem Himmel

bone:

~ idle	stinkfaul
have a ~ to pick with s.b.	mit jdm. ein Hühnchen zu rupfen haben
make no ~s about s.th.	keinen Hehl aus etw. machen

I'm disappointed, I'll make no bones about it.

~ of contention *The time he comes home in the evening has always been a bone of contention between me and my son.*	Zankapfel, Streitobjekt
to feel it in one's ~s	etwas im Gefühl haben
book:	
in my ~	so wie ich die Sache sehe, meiner Meinung nach
suit s.b.'s ~ *The arrangement will suit my book very well.*	jdm. in den Kram passen
go by the ~	sich genau an die Regeln halten
he is in s.b.'s good/bad ~s	jmd. ist gut/schlecht auf ihn zu sprechen
It's a closed ~ to me.	Das ist ein Buch mit sieben Siegeln für mich.
What a turn-up for the ~!	Was für eine Überraschung!
boon:	
a ~ and a blessing	sehr willkommen
a ~ companion	ein guter Kumpel
boot:	
My heart is in my ~s.	Das Herz ist mir in die Hose gerutscht.
The ~ is on the other foot.	Die Sache ist gerade umgekehrt.
~ s.o. out	jdn. hinausschmeißen
born:	
~ to the purple	von königlicher oder aristokratischer Abstammung
~ with a silver spoon in one's mouth *She has never had to worry about money, she was born with a silver spoon in her mouth.*	mit einem silbernen Löffel im Mund geboren sein
~ within the sound of the Bow bells	ein echter Cockney (Einwohner von London)
I was not ~ yesterday.	Ich bin nicht von gestern.
a bosom friend	ein Busenfreund

s.o. can not be bothered with s.th.	etwas interessiert jdn. nicht
bottle:	
to ~ out of s.th. (Sl.)	sich vor etwas drücken
a ~ party	eine Party, bei der die Gäste die Getränke beisteuern
one's bottom drawer	Aussteuer
one's bounden duty	jds. Pflicht und Schuldigkeit
bow:	
~ and scrape	katzbuckeln
~ to the inevitable	sich dem Unausweichlichen fügen
box:	
~ office	Kartenverkauf
on the ~	in der Glotze
to brace oneself	sich auf etwas gefasst machen
brass:	
It's ~-monkey weather!	Es ist saukalt!
the top ~	die militärische Führung
Clearly, the top brass is less than happy with the new policy.	
to get down to ~ tacks	zur Sache kommen
bread:	
~ and butter	Einkommen, Lebensunterhalt
I hate being a mechanic, but it's my bread and butter.	
~ and circuses	Brot und Spiele
break:	
~ away from	Abstand nehmen von
~ cover	aus der Deckung kommen
~ down (s.th.)	1. etwas niederreißen, 2. etwas überwinden, 3. zusammenbrechen
1. The police had to break down the door in order to get into the apartment.	

2. It took a long time to break down his inhibitions.	
3. After the accident, she broke down completely.	
~ new ground	etwas völlig Neues machen, Neuland betreten
The firm broke new ground in computer technology.	
~ the ice	die Stimmung auflockern, das Eis brechen
~ out	ausbrechen
~ the spell	einen Zauber brechen
~-through	ein (revolutionärer) Durchbruch
make a clean breast (of)	etwas offen eingestehen
breath:	
a ~ of fresh air	neu, erfrischend
She has a wonderful personality, just like a breath of fresh air.	
to save one's ~	sich seine Worte sparen
under one's ~	leise, geflüstert
He went away swearing under his breath.	
breathe:	
~ one's last	den letzten Atemzug tun
~ a sigh of relief	Seufzer der Erleichterung
~ down s.b.'s neck	jdm. im Nacken sitzen
I can't work with you breathing down my neck.	
brick:	
come down like a ton of ~s on s.o. (Sl.)	jdn. zur Schnecke machen
The manager came down like a ton of bricks on him for losing the money.	
drop a ~ (Sl.)	einen Schnitzer machen
bridle one's tongue	seine Zunge im Zaum halten

bright and early	früh am Morgen
bring:	
~ about	verursachen, herbeiführen
~ about a change	eine Änderung mit sich bringen
~ into play	ins Spiel bringen
~ o.s. to	sich überwinden
She couldn't bring herself to apologise.	
~ out	zum Vorschein bringen
The crisis brought out the best in him.	
~ s.b. down	jdn. zur Strecke bringen
~ s.b. down to earth	jdn. auf den Boden der Tatsachen zurückholen
~ s.b. in on s.th.	jdn. hinzuziehen
~ s.th. home to s.b.	jdm. etwas klarmachen, erklären
~ s.th. into the open	etwas ans Tageslicht bringen
~ s.b. to his senses	jdn. zur Vernunft bringen
~ s.th. to a close	etwas beenden, zu Ende bringen
~ s.th. to light	etwas aufdecken, ans Tageslicht bringen
~ s.th. up	etwas erwähnen
~ the house down	Zuschauer zu begeistertem Applaus hinreißen
broach the subject	ein Thema zum ersten Mal ansprechen
broad:	
It's about as ~ as it's long.	Das ist gehupft wie gesprungen.
~ly speaking	allgemein gesprochen
to be broke (Sl.)	Pleite sein
a broken marriage	eine kaputte Ehe
a Bronx cheer (Am.)	ein verächtliches Zischen
brook no delay	keine Verzögerung zulassen
to brush s.th. up	etwas auffrischen

brute force	rohe Gewalt
buck up! (Sl.)	Kopf hoch!
to kick the bucket (Sl.)	ins Gras beißen (Sl.)
to buckle down to s.th.	sich hinter etwas klemmen
build:	
~ one's hopes on	seine Hoffnungen auf etwas setzen
~ castles in the air	Luftschlösser bauen
I like to sit in my chair just building castles in the air.	
to bulk large	eine beherrschende Position einnehmen
His impending move to London bulked large, so he did not get a lot of things done.	
bull:	
like a ~ in a china shop	wie ein Elefant im Porzellanladen
go like a ~ at a gate	mit der Tür ins Haus fallen
bully for you (Sl.)	Applaus! Gratuliere!
to bum s.th. off s.o. (Sl.)	etwas von jmd. schnorren
bump:	
~ s.b. off (Sl.)	jdn. um die Ecke bringen
~ into s.b.	jdm. in die Arme laufen
burn:	
~ one's bridges behind one	alle Brücken hinter sich abbrechen
If you leave university now you'll be burning your bridges behind you.	
~ one's boats	alle Brücken hinter sich abbrechen
~ the candle at both ends	sich Tag und Nacht keine Ruhe gönnen, sich übernehmen
~ the midnight oil (Sl.)	bis spät in die Nacht arbeiten

burst:	
~ into laughter/tears	in Lachen/Tränen ausbrechen
~ into flames	in Flammen aufgehen
~ with pride	vor Stolz platzen
bury:	
~ alive	lebendig begraben, von der Außenwelt abschneiden
~ the hatchet	das Kriegsbeil begraben
~ the past	einen neuen Anfang machen
business:	
~ is ~. (Sprichw.)	Geschäft ist Geschäft.
the ~ in hand	das aktuelle Problem
That's none of your ~.	Das geht dich nichts an.
Mind your own ~.	Kümmere dich um deine eigenen Angelegenheiten.
but:	
~ good	gründlich
~ me no ~s!	Keine Widerrede!
These are my orders and I want you to but me no buts about it now!	
I cannot ~ (help him)	ich kann nicht anders als (ihm zu helfen)
the next ~ one	der Übernächste
No ifs and ~s!	Kein Wenn und Aber!
butcher:	
to take a ~'s at s.th. (Sl.)	etwas betrachten, abschätzen
to butt into a conversation (Sl.)	sich ins Gespräch einmischen
butter:	
~ s.b. up	jdm. Honig um den Bart schmieren
She looks as if ~ wouldn't melt in her mouth. (Sl.)	Sie sieht aus, als könne sie kein Wässerchen trüben.
have butterflies in one's stomach	Schmetterlinge im Bauch haben; ein flaues Gefühl haben
I am really nervous about the interview, I have butterflies in my stomach.	

button one's lip (Sl.) — die Klappe halten

buy:

~ a pig in a poke — die Katze im Sack kaufen
~ that (Sl.) — etwas akzeptieren
~ s.th. for a song — etwas ganz billig erstehen
John was thrilled. He had managed to buy a well-preserved copy of a valuable old book for a song.
~ s.b. off — jdn. abfinden
I'm determined to have my rights. I'll not let them buy me off.

by:

~ accident — zufällig
~ all accounts — so weit bekannt ist
~ all means — unbedingt
~ and ~ — allmählich, nach und nach
~ any chance — vielleicht, möglicherweise
~ anybody's standards — aus jeder Sicht, wie auch immer man es betrachtet
~ chance — zufällig
~ common consent — mit allgemeiner Zustimmung, einstimmig
~ courtesy of — durch die freundliche Unterstützung von
~ definition — per Definition, definitionsgemäß
Having obtained a university degree at some point in life does not make you an intellectual by definition.
~ design — absichtlich
~ dint of s.th. — in Folge von, durch
~ fair means or foul — koste es, was es wolle
~ the ~ — übrigens, nebenbei bemerkt
~ the fire — am Kamin, zu Hause
~ a hair's breadth — knapp, um Haaresbreite
The athlete just missed breaking the record by a hair's breadth.
~ all means — in jedem Fall
~ and large — im Großen und Ganzen
~ hook or ~ cook (Sl.) — auf Biegen und Brechen

~ **no means**	auf keinen Fall
~ **the dozen** *He always buys his wine by the dozen.*	im Dutzend
~ **the dozens** *The fans flocked to the concert by the dozens.*	zu Dutzenden
~ **the scruff of the neck** *He grabbed me by the scruff of the neck and threatened to hit me.*	am Kragen, am Schlafittchen
~ **the skin of one's teeth** (Sl.) *I just managed to catch the bus by the skin of my teeth.*	mit Ach und Krach
~ **the sweat of one's brow**	im Schweiße seines Angesichts
~ **way of** *1. You get to London from Dover by way of Ashford.* *2. By way of greeting, he complained about modern railways.* *3. What do you think about relaxing by way of a trip to the continent this year?*	1. (auf dem Weg) über, 2. als, 3. mittels
~ **the way**	im Übrigen, übrigens
~ **word of mouth** *I've only heard by word of mouth that I've got the job, I'm waiting for written confirmation.*	mündlich

C

cake:	
like hot ~s	wie warme Semmeln, sehr schnell
His latest book is selling like hot cakes.	
a piece of ~	einfach, leicht, eine Kleinigkeit
He pretended that going into the lion's cage was a piece of cake.	
that takes the ~ (Sl.)	das ist unglaublich/das Schärfste (iron.)
call:	
~ at s.b.'s house	bei jdm. vorbeischauen
~ for s.b.	nach jdm. rufen, jdn. abholen
~ off s.th.	etwas abblasen
We were going to go to the disco, but decided to call it off.	
~ on s.b.	jdn. besuchen
~ s.b. names	jdn. beschimpfen
~ a spade a spade	die Dinge beim Namen nennen
~ it a day	Feierabend machen
~ to mind	ins Gedächtnis rufen
~ the tune	den Ton angeben
to give s.o. a ~	jdn. anrufen, sich bei jdm. melden
a callow youth	grüner Junge
can[1]:	
~ do! (Sl., altmodisch)	Kein Problem!
~ do worse than	es könnte schlimmer sein, als
~ a duck swim?	Aber klar!
can[2]:	
carry the ~ (Sl.)	die Schuld auf sich nehmen, die Verantwortung übernehmen
candle:	
be not worth the ~	nicht der Mühe wert sein

burn the ~ at both ends *Poor Gary is completely worn out, he has been burning the candle at both ends lately.*	sich überarbeiten, überanstrengen
not fit to hold a ~ to s.o.	jdm. nicht das Wasser reichen können
can't:	
he ~ see beyond the end of his nose *It's not good asking John what went on, he can't see beyond the end of his nose.*	er sieht nicht über den Tellerrand hinaus
one ~ see one's hand in front of one's face	die Hand nicht vor den Augen sehen können
I ~ stand it.	Ich halte es nicht aus. Ich kann es nicht ausstehen.
cap:	
~ in hand	unterwürfig
put on one's thinking ~ (Sl.) *There must be an answer to the problem, I must put on my thinking cap.*	scharf nachdenken
to mark s.o.'s card (Sl.)	jdn. warnen; jdn. belehren
care:	
~ killed the cat. (Sprichw.)	aufmunternd: Nimm es nicht so schwer!
I don't ~.	Das ist mir egal. Meinetwegen.
I couldn't ~ less.	Das ist mir gleichgültig.
carrott and (the) stick	Zuckerbrot und Peitsche
carry:	
~ all before one	sehr erfolgreich sein
~ away	die Beherrschung verlieren
~ conviction	überzeugend sein
~ coals to Newcastle (Brit.)	Eulen nach Athen tragen
~ the day	den Sieg davontragen
~ the point	jdn. überzeugen
~ a torch for s.o.	für jdn. schmachten

~ on *1. Jane, stop carrying on like that, you ought to be ashamed of yourself. 2. Carry on, you're doing just fine!*	1. sich aufführen, 2. weitermachen
~ one's point	andere von seiner Meinung überzeugen
~ s.b. shoulder-high	jdn. auf Händen tragen
~ s.th. too far	es zu weit treiben
~ weight *There's no need to worry about John. What he says carries no weight.*	wichtig sein, Einfluss haben
put the cart before the horse	das Pferd von hinten aufzäumen

case:

as the ~ may be	je nachdem
in any ~	wie dem auch sein mag, in jedem Fall
in ~	im Falle, dass; falls
just in ~	für alle Fälle; nur für den Fall, dass

cash:

be out of ~	nicht gut bei Kasse sein
~ a cheque	einen Scheck einlösen
~ down	Anzahlung
~ in on s.th.	aus etw. Kapital schlagen
for ~	gegen bar

cat:

Has the ~ got your tongue?	Hat es dir die Sprache verschlagen?
have a ~ nap	ein Nickerchen machen
let the ~ out of the bag	ein Geheimnis lüften, die Katze aus dem Sack lassen
put the ~ among the pigeons	Unruhe stiften, für Aufregung sorgen, Wirbel machen
rain ~s end dogs	wie aus Eimern schütten
wait for the ~ to jump	abwarten, wie der Hase läuft

catch:	
~ a cold	sich erkälten
~ it	1. etwas verstehen, mitbekommen 2. Ärger kriegen
1. I didn't catch what he was saying. *2. If you are late again, you will catch it for sure!*	
~ a few rays (Sl.)	sich die Sonne auf den Bauch scheinen lassen.
~ a packet (Sl.)	sein Fett abkriegen
~ at straws	nach jedem Strohhalm greifen
~ me!	Das fällt mir nicht ein!
~ one's death of cold (Sl.)	sich den Tod holen
~ on (Sl.)	gut ankommen, populär werden
~ one's breath	verschnaufen; (vor Schreck) die Luft anhalten
~ sight of s.th.	etwas erblicken
~ s.o.'s eye	die Aufmerksamkeit auf sich lenken
The toy tractor caught the little boy's eye.	
~ s.o. out	jdn. erwischen
~ s.o. red-handed	jdn. in flagranti erwischen
~ up with s.o.	jdn. einholen
cause:	
~ a ripple	Wellen schlagen
~ a stir	Aufsehen erregen
certain:	
make ~	sich vergewissern
That's for ~.	Das ist sicher.
A chain is only as strong as its weakest link. (Sprichw.)	Eine Kette ist nur so stark wie ihr schwächstes Glied.
as different as chalk and cheese	so verschieden sein wie Tag und Nacht
The brothers are as different as chalk and cheese.	

chance:	
~ acquaintance	Zufallsbekanntschaft
~ upon s.th/s.o.	etwas/jdn. zufällig finden
~ would be a fine thing	Schön wär's!
~ one's luck	sein Glück herausfordern
He never takes a ~.	Er geht nie ein Risiko ein.
stand a fair ~	eine gute Chance haben
change:	
~ hands	den Besitzer wechseln, weitergegeben werden
That shop only ever changed hands once.	
~ one's mind	es sich anders überlegen, die Meinung ändern
~ one's colour	erröten
~ course	die Richtung wechseln
~ and decay	natürlicher Verfall der Dinge
~ the face of s.th.	etwas grundlegend verändern
~ gear	die Taktik ändern, das Thema wechseln
~ horses in mid-stream	plötzlich einen anderen Kurs einschlagen
a ~ of heart	Sinneswandel
the ~ of life	Wechseljahre
~ one's tune	seine Ansichten ändern, andere Töne anschlagen
You'll soon change your tune when you hear what is in store for you.	
~ one's ways	seinen Lebenswandel ändern
small ~	Wechselgeld
chapter:	
~ of accidents	eine Reihe von Unfällen
give ~ and verse	genau oder sehr ausführlich zitieren
charge:	
be in ~ of	der Chef sein, die Verantwortung haben
~ $ 5 for	$ 5 berechnen für
free of ~	kostenlos

~ s.th. to s.o. or s.th. *She charged her new car to her father.*	etwas auf Rechnung anderer kaufen
Charity begins at home. (Sprichw.)	Jeder ist sich selbst der Nächste.
chatter like a magpie	geschwätzig sein wie eine Elster
cheap at the price	der Preis ist angemessen
check:	
~ in	(im Hotel) einchecken
~ up *The police are checking up on what we told them.*	überprüfen
cheek:	
~ by jowl	eng zusammen, nebeneinander
What a ~!	Was für eine Frechheit!
cheer:	
~ s.o. up	jdn. aufheitern
~ up!	Kopf hoch!
a chequered career	eine bewegte Laufbahn
chest:	
get s.th. off one's ~ (Brit.) *Thank goodness I've told you. I've been wanting to get that off my chest for a long time.*	sich etwas von der Seele reden
chew:	
~ the cud	wiederkäuen
~ the fat	ein Schwätzchen halten
~ over s.th. (Sl.)	etwas diskutieren, über etwas nachdenken
chicken:	
~-feed (Am./Sl.) *The cost will be chicken-feed in comparison to the gains.*	Peanuts, vernachlässigbar

~ out of s.th. (Sl.)	einen Rückzieher machen, abhauen
It's no good trying to chicken out now, you have agreed to the plan.	
count one's ~ before they're hatched	den Tag vor dem Abend loben, sich zu früh freuen
child:	
a ~ in such matters	unerfahren, naiv
~'s play	ein Kinderspiel
a chink in one's armour	jds. Schwachstelle, wunder Punkt
chip:	
be a ~ off the old block (Sl.)	Der Apfel fällt nicht weit vom Stamm.
have a ~ on one's shoulder	einen Komplex haben
have had one's ~s (Sl.)	erledigt sein, ausgedient haben
chock-a-block	randvoll
chocolate box	ästhetisch angenehm, aber ohne Tiefgang; niedlich
Her pictures are quite nice, pleasant and unoffensive in a chocolate box sort of way.	
choice:	
have Hobson's ~	überhaupt keine Wahl haben
take one's ~	seine Wahl treffen
chop:	
~ and change	rein in die Kartoffeln, raus aus den Kartoffeln
to get the ~	gefeuert werden
chuck it (Sl.)	etwas (hin)schmeißen
be back in circulation	wieder mitmischen
a city slicker (Sl.)	schlitzohriger Großstädter
civvy street (militärischer Sl.)	Zivilleben

clap:	
~ eyes on	zu Gesicht bekommen
I haven't clapped eyes on him for several weeks.	
~-trap	Geschwätz
a clarion call for liberty	ein Ruf nach Freiheit
class distinctions	gesellschaftliche Unterschiede, Klassenunterschiede
clean:	
be ~ out of s.th. (Am./Sl.)	gerade eben ausverkauft sein
~ forget	etwas vollkommen vergessen
make a ~ sweep	reinen Tisch machen
Cleanliness is next to godliness. (Sprichw.)	Ordnung ist das halbe Leben.
clear:	
~ cut	scharf umrissen, eindeutig
with a ~ conscience	mit gutem Gewissen
~ as crystal	ganz offensichtlich
Jack's reason for going to London is as clear as crystal.	
~ the decks	klar Schiff machen
~ of	frei von
The river is clear of weeds and fun to swim in.	
~ off	weggehen, abhauen
~ one's character	jds. Unschuld beweisen
~ one's conscience	Buße tun, sein Gewissen erleichtern
~ one's throat	sich räuspern
~ the air	Missverständnisse aus dem Weg räumen
~ s.th. up	1. deutlich und klar machen, 2. aufräumen
1. I am trying to clear up the misunderstanding. *2. You'll have to clear up your room before you invite your friends.*	
~ up	schöner werden (Wetter)

The weather has cleared up. we can go for a walk.	
to be in the ~ (Sl.)	von einem Verdacht befreit sein
The coast is ~.	Die Luft ist rein.
clench one's teeth	die Zähne zusammenbeißen
clever dick	Klugscheißer
click:	
~ one's heels	die Hacken zusammenschlagen
~ one's tongue	mit der Zunge schnalzen
climate of opinion	die allgemeine Stimmung
climb the wall	die Wände hochgehen
clinch a deal	ein Geschäft abschließen
clip s.b.'s wings	jdm. die Flügel stutzen
cloak and dagger	geheimnisumwittert, mysteriös
He joined the intelligence services expecting a lot of cloak and dagger events, but was disappointed by the seriousness of the work.	
clock:	
It worked like ~work.	Es lief wie am Schnürchen.
work against the ~	gegen die Uhr arbeiten
close:	
a ~d book	ein Buch mit sieben Siegeln, unverständlich, ein Rätsel
Physics is a closed book to me.	
behind ~d doors	hinter verschlossenen Türen
~ one's eyes to s.th.	die Augen vor etwas verschließen
be ~ at hand	in der Nähe sein
~ in on	umzingeln
the days ~ in	die Tage werden kürzer
~ on	dicht bei

at ~ quarters	dicht dran, nahe
~ up shop (Sl.) It's six o'clock, time to close up shop for today.	Feierabend machen
That was a ~ shave! (Sl.) *That was a close shave! The van nearly ran you over.*	Das ging glimpflich aus.
cloud:	
~ one's brain	verwirren
a ~ on the horizon	dunkle Wolken am Horizont
in the ~s	in Gedanken
under a ~	mit angeschlagenem Ruf/Ansehen
live in clover	wie Gott in Frankreich leben
not have a clue *I haven't a clue where he is, ask his mother.*	keine Ahnung haben
turn one's coat	sein Fähnchen nach dem Winde drehen
The cobbler should stick to his last. (Sprichw.)	Schuster, bleib bei deinem Leisten.
cock:	
~ of the walk	Hahn im Korb
~ one's ear	die Ohren spitzen
~-and-bull story	Lügengeschichte
coffee-table book	Bildband
cog in the machine	ein Rädchen im Getriebe
coin:	
~ money *I would not exactly say we are coining money, but we are doing okay so far.*	Geld scheffeln
pay s.b. back in his own ~	es jdm. mit gleicher Münze heimzahlen
the other side of the ~	die Kehrseite der Medaille

cold:	
in ~ blood	kaltblütig, absichtlich
~ comfort	(iron.) schwacher Trost
a ~ fish	eine kalte, unemotionale Person
a ~ fury	kontrollierte Wut
~ hands and a warm heart. (Sprichw.)	Wer kalte Hände hat, der hat ein warmes Herz.
give s.b. the ~ shoulder	jdm. die kalte Schulter zeigen
a ~ snap	Kälteeinbruch
the Cold War	der Kalte Krieg
throw ~ water on s.th.	die Begeisterung dämpfen
collar and tie	ordentlich angezogen
collect one's wits	seine fünf Sinne zusammennehmen
colour:	
come through with flying ~s	einen glänzenden Sieg erringen
have a high ~	rot im Gesicht sein
off ~	nicht ganz fit
show one's true ~s	Farbe bekennen
~ up	rot werden
come:	
~ about	sich ereignen
~ across	1. überqueren, 2. finden, zufällig treffen
1. He came across the road to greet me. *2. Tidying up my room, I came across a couple of old love letters.*	
~ again? (Sl.)	Wie bitte?
~ alive	munter werden
~ along!	Beeil dich!
~ amiss	ungeeignet sein
~ apart at the seams (Sl.)	die Selbstbeherrschung verlieren, ausrasten
~ clean (Sl.)	alles beichten
~ a cropper	stolpern, einen massiven Rückschlag erleiden
~ down on s.o. like a ton of bricks (Sl.)	jdm. über den Mund fahren
~ down with s.th.	an etwas erkranken

John is coming down with the flu, he must go to bed.	
~ **and go**	gelegentlich, mal so, mal so
~ **in handy** (Sl.)	nützlich sein
~ **hell or high water**	egal, wie schwer es sein mag
~ **into line with**	übereinstimmen mit
~ **into the open**	offenbaren, mit etwas herausrücken
You must come into the open and say what you really think.	
~ **off it** (Sl.)	Sag die Wahrheit, tu nicht so.
~ **rain,** ~ **shine**	unter allen Umständen
~ **round**	das Bewusstsein wiedererlangen
~ **to a bad end**	ein böses Ende nehmen
~ **to blows**	sich schlagen
The two brothers came to blows over the girl.	
~ **to grief**	Pech/Unglück haben
He was learning to skate but came to grief at the corner.	
~ **to nothing**	Es wird nichts daraus.
~ **to one's senses**	wieder zu sich kommen
~ **to s.b.'s help**	jdm. zu Hilfe kommen
~ **to the point**	zur Sache kommen
Come to the point, I can't wait all day.	
~ **to a head**	sich zuspitzen (Situation)
~ **to think of it**	wenn ich es mir so überlege
~ **unstuck**	schiefgehen
~ **up in the world**	es zu etwas bringen
Since I started my new job I've really come up in the world.	
~ **up with s.th.**	etwas vorschlagen, sich etwas einfallen lassen
It was Joseph who came up with the idea of moving house.	
~ **what may**	komme was wolle

comic:

~ **opera**	eine Farce

common:

~ **decency**	Anstand

the ~ good	Gemeinwohl
~ ground	gemeinsame Basis
~ herd	die Masse, der Pöbel
~ knowledge	Allgemeinwissen
~ sense	gesunder Menschenverstand
have s.th. in ~ with	etwas gemeinsam haben mit
compliment:	
return the ~	das Kompliment erwidern
fish for ~s	nach Komplimenten fischen, Komplimente erheischen wollen
~s of the season	Grüße zu Weihnachten und zum neuen Jahr
condition:	
on ~ that ...	unter der Bedingung, dass ...
I'll come on condition that I receive a proper invitation.	
out of ~	in schlechter Verfassung
con trick	Schwindel, Beschiss
confirm:	
~ one's worst fears	die schlimmsten Befürchtungen bestätigen
~ed bachelor	überzeugter Junggeselle
confound the prophets	sich entgegen aller Vorhersagen als erfolgreich erweisen
confusion reigns	es herrscht Chaos
conk out (Sl.)	ohnmächtig werden, einschlafen
be well-connected	gute Beziehungen haben
one's conscience pricks one	man fühlt sich schuldig
conspicuous by one's absence	durch Abwesenheit glänzen
contain oneself	sich beherrschen, den Ausdruck starker Emotionen unterdrücken

contradiction in terms	Widerspruch in sich
conversation piece	Ein ungewöhnliches Objekt, das oft zu Gesprächen Anlass gibt; Gesprächsentzünder
cook:	
~ the books (Brit.)	Bücher fälschen
~ s.o.'s goose	jdn. ins Verderben stürzen
That's the way the cookie crumbles. (Am./Sl.)	Das ist der Lauf der Welt.
cool:	
~, calm and collected	vollkommen beruhigt, gelassen
~ customer (Sl.)	ein souveräner Typ, ein gerissener Kerl
~ it! (Am./Sl.)/**Keep ~!** (Brit./Sl.)	Beruhige dich!
~ off	abkühlen
~ down	abkühlen, sich beruhigen
to let s.o. ~ his heels	jdn. warten lassen
cop it	in Schwierigkeiten kommen, bestraft werden
cops and robbers	Räuber und Gendarm
to cope with s.th.	mit etwas klar kommen
corner the market	den Markt beherrschen
The American companies cornered the market in modern art ages ago.	
corridors of power	die Zirkel der Macht in Regierungen, Industrie etc.
cost:	
at all ~s	um jeden Preis
to know to one's ~	aus eigener Erfahrung wissen
~ a packet (Am./Sl.)	extrem teuer sein
~ s.b. dear	jdn. teuer zu stehen kommen
His absent-mindedness cost him dear when he missed the exam date by mistake.	

cough s.th. up. (Sl.)	mit etwas herausrücken
could:	
~ go s.th.?	Hättest du gerne ...?
I am parched – could you go a cup of tea?	
~ cheerfully murder s.b.	wirklich sauer auf jdn. sein
~ swear that	sich ganz sicher sein, dass ...; man hätte geschworen, dass, ...
couldn't:	
~ agree more!	Ganz deiner Meinung!
~ care less!	Das ist mir so etwas von egal!
count:	
~ against s.th.	gegen etwas sprechen
lose ~ of	sich verzählen, den Überblick verlieren
~ on s.b.	auf jdn. zählen
~ s.b. in	jdn. dazuzählen, jdn. beteiligen an
~ me out! (Sl.)	Ohne mich!
~ one's blessings	sich darüber im Klaren sein, wie gut es einem geht
~ the cost	die Vor-und Nachteile gegeneinander abwägen
~ the days	die Tage zählen
~ the pennies	genau rechnen, (häufig auch:) geizig sein
~ sheep	Schäfchen zählen
a country cousin	ein Landei
course:	
in due ~	zu gegebener Zeit
in the ~ of time	im Laufe der Zeit
of ~	natürlich
stay the ~	durchhalten
take it's~	seinen Lauf nehmen
~ of action	weitere Vorgehensweise
~ of history	der Ablauf der Ereignisse
The decision not to sign the treaty after all changed the course of history.	

~ of justice	rechtliche Regeln und Abläufe
to court death	mit seinem Leben spielen
send s.o. to Coventry	jdn. gesellschaftlich ächten/ schneiden
cover: **~ a lot of ground**	1. weit herumkommen, 2. umfassend sein
1. We covered a lot of ground during our holiday in France. *2. His talk covered a lot of ground.*	
~ for s.o.	jdn. schützen
~ one's tracks	seine Spuren verwischen
from ~ to ~	von Anfang bis Ende (Buch)
crack:	
~ a bottle	eine Flasche köpfen
~ a joke	einen Witz erzählen, einen Witz reißen
~ down on s.o.	jdm. gegenüber hart sein
to get ~ing (Sl.)	loslegen
He is ~ing up. (Sl.)	Er dreht durch.
crackerjack	Knaller, Bombe
crafty as a cartload of monkeys	sehr raffiniert
to cramp s.b.'s style *I was overjoyed at seeing her, at the same time her parents' presence rather cramped my style.*	jdm. im Weg sein
a crash course	eine kompakte Unterweisung in kurzer Zeit, Crashkurs
create:	
~ a bad impression	einen schlechten Eindruck machen
~ hell/murder	Ärger machen
creature comforts	leibliches Wohl

credibility gap *The credibility gap opened up by his report was widening all the time.*	Glaubwürdigkeitslücke
to be up the creek	in Schwierigkeiten sein
creep:	
~ and crawl	sich unterwürfig benehmen
~ing paralysis	schleichende Lähmung, Erstarrung
to give s.o. the ~s	jdn. nervös machen
Crime doesn't pay. (Sprichw.)	Verbrechen zahlt sich nicht aus.
crocodile tears	Krokodilstränen
cross:	
~ a person's path	jdm. in die Quere kommen
~ s.b.'s palm with silver *He crossed the fortune teller's palm with silver.*	jdm. Geld geben (für Gefälligkeiten)
~ a bridge when one comes to it *I can't make up my mind on that point now, we'll cross that bridge when we come to it.*	ein Problem lösen
~ one's mind	einfallen
~ one's fingers	Daumen drücken
~ the Great Divide	sterben
~ my heart and hope to die!	Ich schwöre es!
to crown it all	der krönende Abschluss
crowning success	die beste Leistung, Glanzleistung
when the crunch comes	wenn es wirklich ernst wird
to have a crush on s.b.	verknallt sein
the crux of the matter	das wesentlichste Problem

cry:	
~ for the moon	das Unmögliche wollen, nach den Sternen greifen
~ havoc	verwüsten, rücksichtslos gegen jdn. vorgehen
~ one's heart out	sich die Augen ausweinen
~ o.s. to sleep	sich in den Schlaf weinen
~ing over spilt milk	wegen etwas weinen, das nicht zu ändern ist; sich ärgern
~ wolf	falschen Alarm auslösen
crystal clear	glasklar, offensichtlich
a cuckoo in the nest	ein Kuckucksei
off the cuff	improvisiert
a culture vulture	Kulturfanatiker(in)
cup:	
s.b.'s ~ of tea	jds. Fall/Ding sein
Frankly, cricket has never been my cup of tea.	
the ~ that cheers (but not inebriates)	Tee
The cure is worse than the disease. (Sprichw.)	das Mittel ist oft schlimmer als die Krankheit; die Mittel zur Lösung eines Problems sind schlimmer als das Problem selbst
The proponents of the return of capital punishment have clearly failed to grasp that the cure may well be worse than the disease.	
Curiosity killed the cat. (Sprichw.)	Frag nicht so viel! Zu große Neugier treibt den Vogel in die Schlinge
a curtain lecture	Gardinenpredigt
The customer is always right. (Sprichw.)	Der Kunde ist König.

cut:	
~ a fine figure	gut aussehen, elegant sein
~ and dried	1. nicht besonders aufregend, trocken, 2. geplant, vorbereitet
1. His speech was very cut and dried, there was nothing new in it. *2. His plans for leaving were all cut end dried.*	
~ and thrust	schneller Austausch von Argumenten
A lawyer needs to be quick-witted to survive the cut and thrust of the courtroom.	
~ back on s.th.	einschränken, sparen
When the economy is weak the government must cut back on its spending.	
~ in on s.o.	jdn. unterbrechen
~ it rather fine	es gerade noch schaffen
~ off one's nose to spite one's face (Sprichw.)	sich ins eigene Fleisch schneiden
But you love going to the theatre! If you don't go just because you are angry, it'll be cutting off your nose to spite your face.	
~ one's cables	seine Verbindungen beenden
~ s.o. dead	jdn. links liegen lassen, jdn. schneiden
be ~ out for s.th.	das Zeug zu etwas haben, für etwas wie geschaffen sein
~ s.o/s.th. off short	unterbrechen
~ s.o. to the quick	jdn. zutiefst verletzen
~ no ice (Sl.)	keine Wirkung haben, keinen Einfluss haben
It ~s both ways.	Es hat seine Vor- und Nachteile.
a ~ above s.o. (Sl.)	etwas Besseres
a short ~	eine Abkürzung
It is 3 miles to school by road, but there is a short cut through the park.	

D

be a dab hand at s.th. — in etwas besonders tüchtig sein

dagger:
look ~s at s.o. (Sl.) — jdn. mit Blicken töten
at ~s drawn — auf Kriegsfuß stehen, in einem Zustand der offenen Feindschaft

damage:
the ~ is done — das ist nicht mehr zu ändern
What's the ~? — Was kostet der Spaß?

damn:
~ all — absolut nichts; so wenig, dass es der Erwähnung nicht lohnt

He got damn all for his last job, so no wonder he's bitter about the company!

~ and blast! — Verflucht noch eins!
not to give a ~ — sich den Teufel um etwas scheren

I'll be ~ed if I'll … — Ich denke nicht im Traum daran, … zu tun

a damp squib — ein Reinfall

dance:
~ attendance — jdn. den Hof machen
~ to s.b.'s tune — nach der Pfeife von jdm. tanzen

Darby end Joan — ein liebevolles verheiratetes (meist nicht mehr ganz junges) Paar

Say what you like about the Dellameres, I always feel they are a perfect Darby and Joan.

dark:

in the ~ — im Ungewissen
I am completely in the dark concerning his plans.

a ~ horse — ein unbeschriebenes Blatt
I don't know much about John, he's a bit of a dark horse.

a leap in the ~ — ein Sprung ins kalte Wasser
Starting a new job in a foreign country is always a leap in the dark.

keep s.th. ~ — etwas geheim halten

(not) to darken s.b.'s door again — jds. Haus (nie) wieder betreten

dash:

~ s.o.'s hopes — Hoffnungen enttäuschen/zerschlagen
Failing the exam dashed all his hopes of getting a good job.

~ it all! (Sl.) — Verflucht! Verflixt!

~ to pieces — in Stücke schlagen

~ s.th. off — schnell schreiben, schnell erledigen
I'm in a hurry but must just dash off a quick note to my parents.

make a ~ for s.th. — sich stürzen auf, losstürmen

date:

be up to ~ — modern sein, auf dem neuesten Stand sein

~ back to — 1. auf eine Zeit zurückgehen, 2. herrühren
1. This cupboard dates back to the 17th century.
2. His limp dates back to his accident.

Davy Jones's locker — die See als Grab
After all his time at sea he ended up in Davy Jones's locker after all.

dawn:

~ on s.o. — jdm. klar werden

When will it dawn on him that he is talking a lot of nonsense?	
the ~ chorus	das Singen der Vögel am Morgen
day:	
~ of ~s	ein spezieller Tag
at the end of the ~	schließlich
every other ~	jeden zweiten Tag
fall on evil ~s	eine Pechsträhne haben
have a ~ off	einen freien Tag haben
Let's call it a ~!	Schluss für heute! Feierabend!
I'm feeling very tired, let's call it a day and go home.	
make one's ~	jdn. glücklich machen
My ~ is done.	Meine Zeit ist vorbei.
one of these ~s	bald, in den nächsten Tagen
see better ~s	bessere Zeiten sehen (fast immer in der Vergangenheit)
The motorcycle had obviously seen better days.	
This is not my ~.	Das ist heute nicht mein Tag.
the other ~	neulich, vor kurzem
this ~ week	heute in einer Woche
this ~ last week	heute vor einer Woche
to the ~	auf den Tag genau
~ after ~	täglich, Tag für Tag
~ in and ~ out	den lieben langen Tag, dauernd
daylight robbery	überhöhte Preise
dead:	
a ~ loss	ein hoffnungsloser Fall
~ and alive	leblos, desinteressiert
~ and gone	seit langem tot
as ~ as a doornail (Brit.)	mausetot
in the ~ of the night	mitten in der Nacht
The burglers came in the dead of the night.	
~ and buried	tot und begraben, aus und vorbei
That kind of idea is dead and buried.	

a ~ certainty	eine absolut sichere Sache
~ easy	kinderleicht
~ on one's feet	erschöpft
~ tired/beat	todmüde
~ men (Sl.)	leere Flaschen
~ from the neck up	dumm, desinteressiert
~ letter	ein unzustellbarer Brief
~pan	ausdruckslos, ohne sichtbare Reaktion
be ~ to the world	tief und fest schlafen
You must give him a shake to wake him, he's dead to the world.	
~ to s.th.	von etwas nicht betroffen
a ~ weight	eine schwere Bürde
~ to the wide	physisch erschöpft
~ wood	nicht mehr in Gebrauch, veraltet, nutzlos
over my ~ body	nur aber meine Leiche
If that dog comes into the house again, it will be over my dead body.	

deaf:

~ and dumb	taubstumm
turn a ~ ear to s.th.	sich einer Sache gegenüber taub stellen
My mother turned a deaf ear to my pleas for a new dress.	
be ~ as a post	stocktaub sein
It's not good shouting at grandfather, he's as deaf as a post.	

deal:

It's a ~! (Am./Sl.)	Abgemacht!
~ a blow	einen Schlag versetzen
a great ~ of	eine ganze Menge von
~ in s.th.	mit etwas handeln
~ with	sich befassen mit, etwas erledigen
The Managing Director always deals with his post himself.	
It's your ~.	Du bist dran (die Karten zu geben).
no big ~	keine große Sache, unwichtig

dear:	
~ knows	niemand weiß
~ me	Oh je!
~ to s.b.'s heart	von jdm. sehr geliebt oder geschätzt
death:	
one's ~ agony	Todeskampf
~ bed	Sterbebett
~ comes to us all (Sprichw.)	Einmal muss jeder gehen.
at ~'s door	den Tod vor Augen
The priest was called in as the patient was obviously at death's door.	
bore s.o. to ~	jdn. tödlich langweilen
~ warrant	(schriftliches) Todesurteil
to look like ~ warmed up	wie eine wandelnde Leiche aussehen
~ on s.o./s.th. (Am./Sl.)	1. sehr effektiv gegen jdn./etwas, 2. gut/geschickt
1. This new cleaning fluid is just death on all stains. *2. He's just death on the tennis court.*	
a decent sort	ein anständiger Kerl
decide in favour of s.o/s.th.	sich für jdn./eine Sache entscheiden
decline:	
~ and fall	Aufstieg und Niedergang
~ing years	hohes Alter
deep:	
~ in thought	in Gedanken versunken
be in ~ waters	das Wasser bis zum Hals stehen haben
to go off the ~ end	sich aufregen
defeat one's purpose	ein beabsichtigtes Ergebnis stören

deliver the goods	tun, was von einem erwartet wird
delusions of grandeur	Größenwahn
demean oneself *Much as John annoyed me, I was determined not to demean myself by replying in kind.*	sich erniedrigen
den:	
a ~ of iniquity	ein Sündenpfuhl
a ~ of thieves	eine Räuberhöhle
get out of one's depth *The student was out of his depth in discussions on the Middle Ages.*	unsicher werden, ins Schwimmen kommen
dereliction of duty	Pflichtvergessenheit
have designs on s.o.	Absichten in Bezug auf jdn. haben
Desperate diseases require desperate remedies. (Sprichw.)	Der Zweck heiligt die Mittel.
devil:	
The ~ makes work for idle hands. (Sprichw.)	Müßiggang ist aller Laster Anfang.
be between the ~ and the deep blue sea	in der Klemme sitzen, zwischen Hölle und Fegefeuer
The ~ one knows is better than the ~ one doesn't know. (Sprichw.)	Besser ein bekanntes als ein unbekanntes Übel.
The ~ looks after his own.	Diejenigen, die es am wenigsten verdienen, haben das meiste Glück.
a ~ with women	ein Schürzenjäger
devoid of s.th.	ohne etwas

devotion to duty — Pflichtbewusstsein

dice are loaded against s.o. — jds. Chancen sind gering

did he fall or was he pushed? (iron.) — War er selbst schuld an seinem Unglück oder hat jmd. nachgeholfen?

die:

Never say ~! — Nur nicht verzweifeln! Nur nicht nachgeben!

to be dying for s.th. — sich nach etwas sehnen, auf etwas brennen

~ hard — trotz Widerstand bestehen bleiben

~ off — 1. dahinsterben, 2. verschwinden, nachlassen

1. The trees in the wood are dying off.
2. The pain is dying off.

~ away — sich legen/beruhigen

The wind is gradually dying away.

dig:

~ a pit — jdm. eine Grube graben

~ in — 1. (sich) eingraben, 2. sich einstellen auf (Sl.), 3. essen, 4. eine Sache anpacken

1. The wind was so cold the hikers had to dig in for the night halfway up the mountain.
2. We have a lot of points to discuss, better dig in for a long meeting.
3. The hungry man helped himself to a plate of food and dug in.
4. If you're worried about the project's outcome just go ahead and dig in!

~ s.o./s.th. (Am./Sl.) — jdn./etwas mögen

I don't dig that kind of thing at all.

~ s.th. up — 1. herauskramen, 2. aufstöbern, 3. finden

1. Now where did you dig up that piece of gossip?
2. I dug up a recipe tor quiche for a friend of mine.
3. Your boyfriend is very good-looking. Where did you dig him up?

a ding-dong (Sl.) — eine hitzige oder gewalttätige Auseinandersetzung

dip into one's pocket — in die Tasche greifen

dirt:
throw ~ at s.b. — jdn. mit Schmutz bewerfen
The election campaign was unfair. A lot of dirt was thrown at the candidate.
treat s.b. like ~ — jdn. wie Dreck behandeln
My uncle is very unfair to my aunt. He treats her like dirt.

dirty:
to play a ~ trick on s.o. — jdn. reinlegen
a ~ word — ein Fluch oder eine Obszönität
~ works at the crossroads — unangenehme Arbeit, auch: Betrug

one's disappearing act — sich vor etwas drücken, aus dem Staub machen

Now that I have time to take the dog for a walk, that animal has done the disappearing act again!

Discretion is the better part of valour. (Sprichw.) — Vorsicht ist besser als Nachsicht.

a dismal failure — eine totale Enttäuschung

a displaced person — ein Flüchtling

keep s.b. at a distance — jdn. auf Distanz halten
A pretty woman will always have difficulty keeping men at a distance.

do:

~ a flip-flop on s.th. (Am.)	die Meinung ändern
The opposition accused the minister of doing a flip-flop too often.	
~ away with	aus dem Weg räumen, beseitigen, töten
The murderer didn't know how to do away with the body.	
to be ~ne for	erledigt sein
~ in (Sl.)	töten, um die Ecke bringen
~ s.th. (Sl.)	etwas verkaufen
~ s.th. up	etwas renovieren, in Ordnung bringen
~ well with s.b.	gut mit jdm. auskommen
Other people don't like the boss but I do quite well with him.	
nothing ~ing	nichts zu machen
I could ~ with	ich könnte ... gut brauchen
That will ~.	Das geht. Das genügt.
That will do, John. You've had enough ice-cream for today.	
That's easier said than done.	Das ist leichter gesagt als getan.
~ one's (level) best	sein Bestes geben
~ one's own thing (Sl.)	tun was man mag/will
I hate doing things with the crowd, I like to do my own thing.	
~ one's bit (Sl.)	seinen Teil erledigen, seine Pflicht tun
~ s.th. the hard way	etwas ungeschickt anstellen
Don't try to hit that nail in with your shoe, that's doing it the hard way.	
~ the dishes	abspülen
~ s.th. up	etwas reparieren
don't let s.o./s.th. get you down	Lass dich von niemandem/nichts kleinkriegen
Don't look a gift horse in the mouth. (Sprichw.)	Einem geschenkten Gaul schaut man nicht ins Maul.
~s and dont's	Regeln, Richtlinien

dodge the issues	die Auseinandersetzung mit einem Problem vermeiden

dog:	
the ~ days	die heißen Tage im Sommer
~-eared	Eselsohren, geknickte Ecken in Buch- oder Heftseiten o. ä.
~ eat ~	rücksichtsloser Konkurrenzkampf
Every ~ has its day.	Ein blindes Huhn findet auch einmal ein Korn.
go to the ~s (Sl.)	vor die Hunde gehen
a ~s dinner	in Unordnung
lead a ~'s life	ein Hundeleben führen
Let sleeping ~s lie.	Schlafende Hunde soll man nicht wecken.
a Don Juan	ein Herzensbrecher
donkey's years	lange Zeit
dot:	
~ and carry	sich mühsam oder unsicher bewegen
~ the i's (and cross the t's)	sehr sorgfältig sein
on the ~	auf die Sekunde genau
double:	
a ~ agent	ein Doppelagent
~ quick	so schnell wie möglich
doubt:	
beyond a ~/without a ~	zweifellos
Without a doubt, that's the best cake I have ever tasted.	
in ~	unsicher
If in doubt, follow your instincts.	
shadow of a ~	leichte Ungewissheit
The judge said he did not have a shadow of a doubt about the prisoner's guilt.	
down:	
~ and out	fertig sein
~ at (the) heel(s)	schäbig, heruntergekommen
~ in the dumps (Sl.)	traurig, deprimiert

When you're feeling down in the dumps, the best thing to do is treat yourself to something.	
~ on one's luck	vom Pech verfolgt sein
go ~ the drain	in die Binsen gehen, für die Katz' sein
~ to earth	mit beiden Beinen auf dem Boden
to be ~ to s.o. (Sl.)	für jdn. zuständig sein
have a ~ on s.b.	jdn. auf dem Kieker haben
He's had a down on me ever since I won the prize.	
~ memory lane	nostalgische Erinnerungen
a ~ payment	eine Anzahlung
~ tools	mit einer Arbeit aufhören, häufig: zu Beginn eines Streiks

drag:

~ one's feet	sich dahinschleppen, langsam machen
If you drag your feet you'll not get the contract.	
~ s.th. out	in die Länge ziehen
~ on	(sich) in die Länge ziehen
The talk was boring and dragged on for hours.	

down the drain	im Eimer

draw:

~ in one's horns (Sl.)	sich krumm legen müssen, sparen
~ a blank	eine Niete ziehen, nicht weiterkommen
~ one's last breath	seinen letzten Atemzug tun
~ s.b.'s attention to	jds. Aufmerksamkeit lenken auf
~ s.b. into s.th.	jdn. in eine Sache hineinziehen
~ the line at	die Grenze ziehen bei
~ s.th. to a close	etwas zu Ende bringen, beschließen
back to the ~ing board	nochmal von vorne
The days are ~ing in.	Die Tage werden kürzer.
~ it mild	sein Benehmen oder seine Aussagen mäßigen

~ a moral	eine Lehre aus etwas ziehen
~ s.b.'s teeth	jdm. die Mittel nehmen, mit denen er Schaden anrichten könnte
dread the moment	ein Ereignis mit Schrecken erwarten
dress:	
~ing-down	eine Standpauke
~ed to kill (Sl.)	aufgetakelt wie eine Fregatte, sehr fein angezogen, herausgeputzt
~ the part	sich passend für einen Anlass kleiden
~ rehearsal	Generalprobe
in dribs and drabs	tropfenweise, häppchenweise
drink:	
~ the cup of sorrow	großes Leid ertragen
~ like a fish	wie ein Loch saufen
drive:	
~ a hard bargain	harte Bedingungen stellen
~ a wedge between	einen Keil treiben zwischen
~ into a corner	in die Ecke treiben
~ to despair	zur Verzweiflung bringen
~ s.o. nuts (Am./Sl.)	jdn. wahnsinnig machen
The sound of his voice is driving me nuts.	
~ s.o. crazy/mad/potty (Brit./Sl.)	jdn. auf die Palme bringen
~ at s.th.	auf etwas hinauswollen
You know what I'm driving at.	
~ s.th. home to s.o.	jdm. etwas klar machen
~ s.o. up the wall (Sl.)	jdn. verrückt machen
One day, all my troubles will drive me up the wall.	
drop:	
~ by ~	tropfenweise
~ by	vorbeischauen
~ in	unerwartet vorbeikommen
~ it! (Sl.)	Lass das!

a ~ in the ocean	ein Tropfen auf dem heißen Stein
~ a brick (Sl.)	ins Fettnäpfchen treten
~ names	in penetranter Weise mit sozialen Kontakten angeben
~ dead! (Sl.)	Scher dich zum Teufel!
~ off (to sleep)	einnicken, einschlafen
~ s.o.	jdn. fallen lassen
~ s.o. a line	jdm. schreiben
~ one's aitches (Sl.)	das „H" beim Sprechen unterdrücken (Zeichen einer niedrigen sozialen Herkunft)
drown one's sorrows (Sl.)	die Probleme im Alkohol ertränken
John is trying to drown his sorrows with a bottle of whisky.	
a drug on the market	ein schwer verkäuflicher Artikel
drum s.th. into s.b.	jdm. etwas einhämmern
as drunk as a lord (Sl.)	stockbesoffen, sternhagelvoll
dry:	
~ up! (Sl.)	Halts Maul!
a ~ run	ein Probedurchlauf, Test
duck:	
take to s.th. like a ~ to water	in seinem Element sein
like a dying ~ in a thunderstorm (Brit./Sl.)	wie der Ochse vor dem Berg, keine Ahnung haben
due:	
~ to	aufgrund
give the devil his ~	dem Kaiser geben, was des Kaisers ist
in ~ time	zur rechten Zeit
stand there like a stuffed dummy (Sl.)	wie Ölgötzen dastehen

to dump s.o.	jdn. loswerden
dust:	
~ of ages	die zerstörerischen Effekte der vergehenden Zeit
bite the ~ (Sl.)	ins Gras beißen
throw ~ in s.o.'s eyes	jdm. Sand in die Augen streuen
Dutch:	
~ courage (Sl.) *He had a couple of drinks at the bar to give him Dutch courage to face his wife.*	angetrunkener Mut
to go ~	eine Rechnung teilen
a ~ treat	ein geselliges Ereignis, bei dem jeder Teilnehmer seine eigenen Kosten trägt
duty:	
~-bound to do s.th.	verpflichtet
~ call	Pflichtbesuch
dyed-in-the-wool	durch und durch, mit tiefsitzenden und unwandelbaren Überzeugungen

E

each:	
~ and every	jeder einzelne
~ according to his taste	jeder wie er mag
an eager beaver	Streber, Enthusiast
ear:	
be all ~s	ganz Ohr sein
be up to one's ~s in work	bis über beide Ohren in Arbeit stecken
bend s.o.'s ~ (Sl.)	jdn. vollquatschen
fall on deaf ~s	tauben Ohren predigen
give one's ~s for s.th.	den rechten Arm für etwas geben
go in at one ~ and out at the other	zum einen Ohr hinein, zum anderen wieder hinaus
(play) by ~	1. nach Gehör spielen, 2. improvisieren
1. She plays the piano entirely by ear. *2. I haven't decided yet what to tell him, I'll play it by ear.*	
a flea in the ~ (Sl.)	(unangenehme) Wahrheiten
A salesman came to the door but I sent him away with a flea in his ear.	
turn a deaf ~	nicht auf etwas hören
He turned a deaf ear to all advice.	
keep an ~ to the ground	Augen und Ohren offen halten
pin back s.o.'s ~s	jdn. übers Ohr hauen
pin back one's ~s	aufmerksam zuhören
Just pin back your ears and listen to what I've got to tell you.	
early:	
The ~ bird catches the worm. (Sprichw.)	Wer zuerst kommt, mahlt zuerst. Morgenstund hat Gold im Mund.
~ days	der Beginn von etwas
be ~ days yet	es ist noch zu früh, etwas dazu zu sagen

She seems rather overwhelmed with her new responsibility. – Oh come on, it is early days yet!

earn:	
~ an honest penny	Geld mit ehrlicher Arbeit verdienen
~ one's living	sich seinen Lebensunterhalt verdienen
ease:	
~ s.b.'s mind	jdn. beruhigen
at ~	zwanglos, bequem
~ off s.th.	1. sich befreien von, 2. erleichtern
1. He eased off his shoes gently as his feet were sore.	
2. They eased off his task.	
~ s.b. of his wallet	jdn. um die Brieftasche erleichtern
feel ill at ~	sich unbehaglich/nicht wohl in seiner Haut fühlen
easier said than done	leichter gesagt als getan
East or West, home is best. (Sprichw.)	Zu Hause ist es doch am schönsten.
easy:	
~ come, ~ go. (Sprichw.)	Wie gewonnen, so zerronnen.
~ does it! (Sl.)	Lass dir Zeit! Vorsicht!
~ on the eye	gefällig, schön anzusehen
~ game	leichte Beute
~ in one's mind	entspannt, beruhigt
Your mother will not be easy in her mind until you have called her!	
~ money	schnell verdientes Geld
on ~ terms	zu günstigen Bedingungen
Take it ~!	Immer mit der Ruhe!
~ to come by	leicht zu finden
A good friend is not easy to come by.	
in ~ circumstances	finanziell gesichert

eat:	
~ away	1. nagen (an), langsam entfernen, 2. ärgern, Sorge machen
1. The sea has eaten away much of the shore. *2. Fear of not passing the exam was eating away at her.*	
~ humble pie (Sl.)	sich demütigen
~ like a bird/sparrow (Sl.)	essen wie ein Spatz, nur kleine Portionen essen
~ one's words	seine Worte zurücknehmen
~ out of s.o.'s hands	jdm. aus der Hand fressen
~ out	essen gehen
~ like a horse (Sl.)	essen wie ein Scheunendrescher
No wonder he's fat, he eats like a horse.	
~ s.b. alive for breakfast	jdn. leicht bezwingen können
~ s.b. out of house and home	jdm. die Haare vom Kopf fressen
~ oneself sick	essen, bis einem schlecht wird
~ one's head off	viel essen
~ one's heart out	sehr traurig sein
John ate his heart out when he had to leave home.	
~ until it comes out of one's ears	essen, bis es einem aus den Ohren wieder rauskommt
edge:	
be on ~	nervös sein, gereizt sein
have an ~ on one's appetite	hungrig sein
set one's teeth on ~	jdn. nervös machen
take the ~ off s.th.	einer Sache die Wirkung nehmen
eff and blind (Sl.)	fluchen
egg:	
as sure as ~s is ~s (Sl.)	so sicher wie das Amen in der Kirche; ganz sicher; man kann sich drauf verlassen

~ s.o. on *The boy only threw the stone because the others egged him on.*	jdn. ermutigen
have one over eight (Sl.)	einen über den Durst trinken
either way	je nachdem
elbow:	
~ one's way	sich hindurchdrängen, sich durchboxen
~ out	vertreiben, verdrängen
have at one's ~	bei der Hand haben
an elder statesman	jmd., der ein Amt lange innegehabt hat und nach wie vor konsultiert wird
at the eleventh hour	fünf vor zwölf, in letzter Minute, kurz bevor es zu spät ist
end:	
~ one's days	seinen Lebensabend verbringen
~ to ~	aneinander gelegt oder gestellt
the ~ of the rainbow	der mystische Ort, an dem alle Wünsche in Erfüllung gehen
come to an ~	enden
get hold of the wrong ~ of the stick	etwas in den falschen Hals bekommen
make ~s meet	mit etwas auskommen
My hair stands on ~.	Die Haare stehen mir zu Berge.
put an ~ to s.th.	einer Sache ein Ende bereiten/machen
~ in *The path ends in a road.*	münden
~ up in *You'll end up in jail.*	enden
All's well that ~s well. (Sprichw.)	Ende gut, alles gut.
to no ~	zwecklos
the enemy at the gates	die bedrohliche Präsenz des Gegners

engage:	
be ~d in	beschäftigt sein mit
~ in politics	sich in der Politik engagieren
be ~d	verlobt sein
~ in small talk	Belangloses reden
The English dearly love a lord. (Sprichw.)	Die Engländer schätzen sozialen Status.
enough:	
~ is ~!	Genug! Schluss damit!
~ is as good as a feast. (Sprichw.)	Allzuviel ist ungesund.
~ and to spare	mehr als genug, reichlich
~ of a fool to do s.th.	dumm genug, etwas zu tun
~ to go round	genug für alle, reichlich
enter:	
~ one's mind/head	in den Sinn kommen
~ into s.th.	etwas anfangen, sich auf etwas einlassen
~ the fray	sich ins Getümmel stürzen
entertain the idea	sich mit etwas beschäftigen
one's entrances end exits	wie jmd. kommt und geht
To err is human (to forgive devine). (Sprichw.)	Irren ist menschlich.
error:	
the ~ of s.b.'s ways	jds. Fehlverhalten
Having realized the errors of his ways, he went back to apologize.	
an ~ of judgement	Fehleinschätzung
escape attention	übersehen werden
eternal triangel	Dreiecksverhältnis
even:	
~ and anon	ziemlich regelmäßig
get ~ with s.o.	es jdm. heimzahlen

ever:

~ more	mit der Zeit zunehmend
~ so	sehr, viel

every:

~ bit as bad	in jeder Hinsicht so schlecht
~ cloud has a silver lining. (Sprichw.)	Nach Regen folgt Sonnenschein. Wo Schatten ist, ist auch Licht.
~ dog has his day. (Sprichw.)	Auch ein blindes Huhn findet einmal ein Korn. Jeder hat mal Glück/eine Chance.
~ now and then	hin und wieder, dann und wann
~ other day	jeden zweiten Tag
~ single one	jeder Einzelne
~ man has his price. (Sprichw.)	Jeder Mann ist käuflich.

everything:

~ but the kitchen sink (Brit./Sl.)	absolut alles
~ from soup to nuts (Am./Sl.)	absolut alles
~ the heart could desire	was man sich nur wünschen könnte
~ under the sun	alles

evil eye	der böse Blick
The exception proves the rule. (Sprichw.)	Ausnahmen bestätigen die Regel.
the expectation of life	Lebenserwartung
expense is no object	Geld spielt keine Rolle
extremes meet	unterschiedliche Positionen prallen aufeinander

In the big cities of today, extremes of wealth and poverty meet at every corner.

eye:

the ~ of the storm	das Auge des Sturms; das Zentrum einer gefährlichen Situation

an ~ for an ~	Auge um Auge
keep an ~ on s.th.	etwas im Auge behalten
make s.b. open his ~s	jdm. die Augen öffnen
my ~!	Unsinn!
never take one's ~s off s.th.	die Augen nicht abwenden
private ~	Privatschnüffler
see ~ to ~	übereinstimmen
with an ~ to	mit Rücksicht auf

eyebrow:

be up to one's ~s in work/debt	bis über beide Ohren in Arbeit/ Schulden stecken.
raise one's ~s	die Stirne runzeln

F

face:	
~ to ~	von Angesicht zu Angesicht, Auge in Auge
~ the music (Sl.) *The boy broke the window and had to face the music when his father came home.*	Zorn über sich ergehen lassen
be ~d with	mit etwas konfrontiert werden/sein
~ up to a failure	einer Niederlage ins Gesicht sehen
~ down	mit dem Gesicht nach unten
fly in the ~ of s.th.	sich einer Sache widersetzen
have the ~ to do s.th.	die Stirn haben, etwas zu tun
in the ~ of death	im Angesicht des Todes
on the ~ of it	auf den ersten Blick, anscheinend
place a ~	jdn. einordnen
pull a ~ at s.o.	Grimassen schneiden
put on a brave ~	sich nichts anmerken lassen
save one's ~	sein Gesicht wahren
show one's ~ *I hate family gatherings, but I must at least show my face.*	sich sehen lassen
take s.th. at ~ value	etwas für bare Münze nehmen
keep a straight ~ *It was very difficult to keep a straight face as the clown performed his tricks.*	ernst bleiben, nicht lachen
fact:	
as a matter of ~	in der Tat, tatsächlich
know s.th. for a ~	etwas genau wissen
~ or fiction	Tatsache oder Erfindung
the ~ of the matter	der entscheidende Aspekt
the ~ remains	es trifft nach wie vor zu
~s and figures	belegte Tatsachen oder Ergebnisse

let the ~s speak for themselves	die Tatsachen sprechen für sich, die Ergebnisse bedürfen keiner weiteren Erläuterung
Faint heart never won fair lady. (Sprichw.)	Frisch gewagt ist halb gewonnen.
fair:	
~-weather friend	ein Freund, der sich in schlechten Tagen zurückzieht
~ do's	gerechte Behandlung oder Beurteilung
~ enough! (Sl.)	Einverstanden!
~'s ~	man muss gerecht sein
~ play	anständiges Verhalten
the ~ sex	das schöne Geschlecht
~ to middling	es geht so, ganz in Ordnung
The party was not really good, only fair to middling.	
~ and square	offen und ehrlich, unzweideutig
with one's own ~ hands	mit den eigenen Händen
Did you cook dinner yourself? – With my own fair hands!	
fairy:	
a ~ godmother	gute Fee
~ tale	Märchen, Lügengeschichte
fall:	
~ all over s.o. (Sl.)	um jdn. viel Aufhebens machen
My friend falls all over my daughter whenever she comes to visit.	
~ back on s.o./s.th.	jdn. um Hilfe bitten, auf etwas zurückgreifen
~ down on the job	etwas nicht richtig machen, mit einer Arbeit nicht zurechtkommen
~ flat on one's face (Sl.)	auf die Nase fallen, ohne Erfolg sein
~ for s.o. (Sl.)	sich verlieben
a ~ guy	Sündenbock

~ on deaf ears	auf taube Ohren stoßen
~ on one's feet	auf die Füße fallen (wie eine Katze)
~ over backwards to do s.th.	sich beinahe überschlagen, etwas zu tun
~ into place	in Ordnung kommen, klar werden
When he told me his story, all the facts I had known before fell into place.	
~ out with s.o.	sich mit jdm. zanken/überwerfen
~ short of s.th.	schlechter als erwartet
~ through	nichts werden, ins Wasser fallen
Our plans for a holiday in Spain fell through, we had no money.	
false:	
~ alarm	Fehlalarm
~ modesty	falsche Bescheidenheit
make a ~ move	einen Fehler machen
fame and fortune	Ruhm und Reichtum
Familiarity breeds contempt. (Sprichw.)	Zu große Vertrautheit erzeugt Verachtung.
family:	
~ likeness	Familienähnlichkeit
~ man	Familienvater
~ planning	Geburtenkontrolle
~ tree	Stammbaum
fancy:	
~ one's chances at s.th.	sich bei etwas gute Chancen ausrechnen
~ s.o. (Sl.)	jdn. attraktiv finden
far:	
~ afield	weit weg
~ and away	bei Weitem
He is far and away the most distinguished actor of his generation.	

~ away	geistesabwesend
~ be it from me to interfere	es liegt mir fern, mich einzumischen
~-fetched	an den Haaren herbeigezogen, weit hergeholt
~ from it!	überhaupt nicht!
~ gone	weit fortgeschritten
~ and near	weit und breit
~ removed from s.th.	sehr anders als
a ~ cry from s.th.	weit davon entfernt sein
as ~ as that goes	was das angeht
not to trust s.o. as ~ as one can throw him	jdm. nicht über den Weg trauen
after a fashion	mehr schlecht als recht, in gewisser Weise

fast:

~ asleep	in tiefem Schlaf
~ bind, ~ find. (Sprichw.)	Wohl aufgehoben ist gut gefunden.
a ~ buck	schnell verdientes Geld
~ and furious	aufgeregt, unruhig
a ~ worker	jmd., der schnell Kontakt zum anderen Geschlecht aufnimmt

fat:

a ~ lot of good	nutzlos
a ~ price	ein hoher Preis
the ~ years and the lean years	fette und magere Jahre
the ~ is in the fire	der Teufel ist los

father:

a ~ figure	Vaterfigur
~ and mother of a row	eine besonders hitzige Auseinandersetzung

fault:

The ~ is in ourselves, not in our stars. (Sprichw.)	Der Mensch schafft sich sein Schicksal selbst.
to a ~	übertrieben

favour:	
in ~ of	zugunsten von
stand high in s.o.'s ~	bei jdm. in besonderer Gunst stehen, gut angeschrieben sein
Would you do me a ~?	Können Sie mir einen Gefallen tun?
feast:	
a ~ for the eyes	eine Augenweide
a ~ of talent	ein Überfluss an Begabung
feather:	
a ~ in one's cap	eine Ehre, eine Belohnung
John earned a feather in his cap by winning the race.	
~ one's nest	seine Schäfchen ins Trockene bringen
to be fed up with s.o./s.th. (Sl.)	etwas/jdn. dick haben, genug von etwas/jdm. haben
Feed a cold and starve a fever. (Sprichw.)	Bei einer Erkältung soll man viel, bei Fieber wenig essen.
feel:	
~ free to do s.th.	das Gefühl haben, man darf etwas tun
Please feel free to borrow the book, I have read it.	
~ out of place	sich fehl am Platz fühlen
~ like doing s.th.	Lust haben, etwas zu tun
~ for s.o.	es jdm. nachfühlen können
~ one's oats	in Hochstimmung sein
~ one's way	sich seinen Weg suchen
Sensing the opposition to their plans, they were feeling their way towards a solution.	
~ s.th. in one's bones	etwas im Gefühl haben
~ the draught	unangenehme Veränderungen spüren (häufig: finanziell)
~ the pinch	Mangel spüren
~ up to s.th.	sich einer Sache gewachsen fühlen

fellow feeling	Unterstützung, Sympathie
The female of the species is more deadly than the male. (Sprichw.)	Frauen sind gefährlicher als Männer.
fence:	
come off the ~	sich für eine Seite entscheiden
sit on the ~	sich nicht entscheiden wollen
the festive season	die Weihnachtstage
few:	
~ and far between	selten, rar, sehr wenig
a ~ home truths	eine klare und direkt geäußerte Kritik
fiddle:	
a face as long as a ~	ein enttäuschtes Gesicht
play second ~	die zweite Geige spielen
~ around with s.th.	an etwas herumspielen
~ while Rome burns	sich in einer kritischen Situation unpassend benehmen
a field day	ein Tag voll erfreulicher Tätigkeit
fight:	
~ the good ~	entschlossen für etwas eintreten
~ like Kilkenny cats	so lange kämpfen, bis beide Seiten zerstört sind
~ like a tiger	wild kämpfen
~ a losing battle	sich um eine aussichtslose Sache bemühen
~ tooth and nail	unter Einsatz aller Mittel kämpfen
~ing fit	einsatzbereit, gesund
~ing talk	Herausforderung
a figment of the imagination	Hirngespinst
figure:	
~ out (Am./Sl.)	schätzen, erraten
a ~ of fun	Witzfigur

filthy lucre	schnöder Mammon
find:	
~ a better hole	sich verbessern
~ one's feet	zurechtkommen
After a year in the job I'm beginning to find my feet.	
~ one's vocation	seine Berufung finden, die geeignete Aufgabe für sich finden
~ s.th. wanting	etwas als nicht ausreichend beurteilen
~ one's way	ankommen, finden
~ing is keeping. (Sprichw.)	Wer etwas findet, darf es auch behalten.
fine:	
a ~ body of men	eine gute Truppe
~ and dandy	wunderbar, prima
Everything would be fine and dandy if only he could get the car started in time.	
~ feathers make ~ birds. (Sprichw.)	Kleider machen Leute
a ~ kettle of fish	ein schönes Schlamassel
a ~ thing	eine gute Sache
a ~ time (iron.)	zu spät, zum falschen Zeitpunkt
Six o'clock in the morning is a fine time for ringing somebody, you know!	
~ words butter no parsnips. (Sprichw.)	Nette Worte alleine helfen nicht weiter!
one's ~r feelings	die bessere Seite der menschlichen Natur
the ~r points of something	Details
the ~st hour	der wichtigste Augenblick im Leben
finger:	
have a ~ in the pie (Sl.)	die Hand im Spiel haben
His ~s are all thumbs. / He's all ~s and thumbs.	Er hat zwei linke Hände.
He won't raise a ~.	Er wird keinen Finger krumm machen.

put one's ~ on it	seinen Finger auf die Wunde legen
twist s.b. round one's little ~	jdn. um den kleinen Finger wickeln
finish:	
the ~ed product	Endergebnis
~ing touches	die letzten Korrekturen
fire:	
get ~d	entlassen werden
get on like a house on ~	dicke Freunde sein
~ away!	Schieß los!
have got ~ coming out of one's ears	etwas nicht mehr hören können
play with ~	mit dem Feuer spielen
firm:	
with a ~ hand	mit eiserner Hand
a ~ offer	ein sicheres Angebot
first:	
~ and foremost	zunächst einmal, vor allem anderen
~ and last	wenn man alles berücksichtigt
~ thing in the morning	als erstes am Morgen, als allererstes
~ thing one knows	ehe man es sich versieht
~ cousin to s.th.	sehr ähnlich
the ~ fine rapture	die erste Freude an etwas Neuem, die nicht lange andauert
~ things ~	die wichtigsten Dinge zuerst
the ~ impression	der erste Eindruck
at ~ sight	auf den ersten Blick
~ come ~ served. (Sprichw.)	Wer zuerst kommt, mahlt zuerst.
The first day a guest, the third day a pest.	Am ersten Tag ein Gast, am dritten Tag eine Last.
from ~ to last	die ganze Zeit
From first to last he never treated his wife fairly.	
fish:	
a fine kettle of ~ (Sl.)	ein schöner Schlamassel

~ for s.th.	nach etwas angeln
a ~ out of water	in ungewohnter Umgebung
have other ~ to fry	Wichtigeres zu tun haben
That's a bit ~y!	Das ist nicht ganz geheuer/legal.
a fisherman's story	Seemannsgarn
fit:	
~ for human consumption	essbar
~ like a glove	genau passend
a ~ of laughter	intensives Gelächter
~ and proper	ordentlich
give s.b. a ~	jdm. einen Schock versetzen
be ~ as a fiddle	gesund sein wie ein Fisch im Wasser
in ~s and starts	schubweise
~ the bill	angemessen, passend
It's not ~ for her.	Es schickt sich nicht für sie.
throw a ~ (Sl.)	einen Anfall kriegen
fix:	
~ s.o. up with s.th.	jdm. etwas besorgen
a ~ed idea	eine fixe Idee, Zwangsvorstellung
be flabbergasted (Sl.)	platt sein
flash:	
a ~ in the pan	ein Strohfeuer
a ~ Harry	ein Lackaffe
flat:	
to be singing ~	falsch singen
~ out (Sl.)	klar und deutlich
They told me flat out that they were reporting me to the police.	
a ~ voice	ausdruckslose Stimme
that's ~	damit kein Zweifel entsteht
flay s.b. alive	jdn. ernsthaft bestrafen
fleet of foot	leichtfüßig; in der Lage, sich schnell zu bewegen

Being rather fleet of foot, I managed to get off the road just in time.

flesh:

~ and blood	Fleisch und Blut
neither ~, fowl nor good red herring	weder Fisch noch Fleisch
put on ~	dick werden
make s.o.'s ~ creep	jdm. eine Gänsehaut einjagen
~ s.th. out	auswalzen, anschaulich machen, mit Details versehen

The plan is good but now you must flesh it out.

flex one's muscles	die Muskeln spielen lassen
have a fling (Sl.)	das Leben genießen (sich gehen lassen)
flip one's lid (Am./Sl.)	plötzlich wütend werden
flog a dead horse (Brit./Sl.)	etwas für nichts und wieder nichts tun
flood the market	den Markt überfluten
flora and fauna	Flora und Fauna
a Florence Nightingale	eine engagierte Krankenschwester
flourish like the green bay tree	blühen und gedeihen

flower:

~ power	Sammelbegriff für die Ideologie der Hippiebewegung
~ children	Blumenkinder, Hippies

fly:

~ the coop	abhauen
~ high	ehrgeizig sein
~ into a rage	in Wut geraten

~ off the handle	die Beherrschung verlieren, aus der Haut fahren
a ~ in the ointment (Sl.)	ein Haar in der Suppe
~-by-night	unzuverlässig(er) Mensch
a ~ing start	ein guter Anfang
a ~ing visit	ein sehr kurzer Besuch
get off to a ~ing	glänzend wegkommen, (fig.) einen glänzenden Start haben
The bird has flown. (Sl.)	Der Vogel ist ausgeflogen.
There are no flies on him.	jmd. ist nicht dumm
fob s.o. off with s.th.	jdm. etwas andrehen
I asked for butter and will not be fobbed off with margarine.	
follow:	
~ in s.b.'s footsteps	in jds. Fußstapfen treten
~ one's nose (Sl.)	immer der Nase nach, geradeaus gehen
~ one's own bent	tun, was man will
~ one's suit	es jdm. gleichtun
~ s.b.'s example	jdn. nachahmen
~ s.b.'s lead	jds. Vorbild oder Beispiel folgen
~ suit	genau das gleiche tun, wie der Vorgänger
fond:	
a ~ farewell	Abschied
in the ~ hope	in der ungerechtfertigten Hoffnung, dass
food:	
~ to s.b.	was jdn. erfreut
Jack's difficulties were food to his competitors.	
~ to the gods	sehr gut
~ for thought	etwas stimmt nachdenklich
fool:	
a ~'s errand	eine sinnlose Sache
A ~ and his money are soon parted. (Sprichw.)	etwa: Ein Narr wird immer pleite sein.

live in a ~'s paradise	in trügerischer Sicherheit leben
make a ~ of o.s.	sich zum Narren machen
No ~ like an old ~. Sprichw.)	Alter schützt vor Torheit nicht.

foot:

be (back) on one's feet	(wieder) auf den Beinen sein
have one ~ in the grave	mit einem Fuß im Grab stehen
~ the bill	die Rechnung bezahlen
have feet of clay	eine verborgene Schwäche haben, auch nur ein Mensch sein
He may be a dictator, but his feet are of clay.	
put one's ~ down	entschlossen handeln, einschreiten
When the girl wanted to stay late at a party, her father put his foot down.	
put one's ~ in it	ins Fettnäpfchen treten

footloose and fancy-free	ungebunden

for:

~ ages	seit ewigen Zeiten
~ one	zum Beispiel
~ all I care	Es ist mir egal.
They can all lose their jobs, for all I care.	
~ all I know	so viel ich weiß
~ all the difference it makes	Wenn man bedenkt, was für einen geringen Unterschied es macht
~ all one's efforts	trotz aller Bemühungen
~ all the world to see	so dass es jeder sehen kann
~ chicken feed (Am./Sl.)	für 'nen Appel und ein Ei, für fast gar nichts, für ein paar Pfennige
~ dear life	entschlossen
~ ever	für immer
~ fear of s.th.	aus Angst vor
~ good	für immer
~ hours on end	stundenlang
~ sure	gewiss

~ the fun of it (Sl.)	nur aus Spaß
~ the time being	zunächst
forbidden:	
~ fruit is sweetest. (Sprichw.)	Verbotene Früchte schmecken am besten.
~ ground	ein Areal, das man nicht betreten darf
force:	
a ~ to be reckoned with	ein Faktor, den man in Betracht ziehen muss
~ s.b.'s hand	jdn. dazu zwingen, etwas zu tun
by ~ of arms	mit militärischen Mitteln
~ of habit	die Macht der Gewohnheit
a foregone conclusion	ein vorhersehbares Ende
forever and a day	für immer und ewig
Forewarned is forearmed. (Sprichw.)	Gefahr erkannt, Gefahr gebannt.
forget:	
~ more about s.th. than s.b. else ever knew	einen deutlichen Wissensvorsprung in einer Sache haben
forgive:	
~ and forget	vergeben und vergessen
~ s.b. his trespasses	jdm. seine Schuld vergeben
fork money out (Sl.)	(etwas unwillig) bezahlen
a forlorn hope	eine sehr schwache Hoffnung
Fortune favours fools. (Sl.)	Mancher hat mehr Glück als Verstand.
forty winks	ein Nickerchen
foul:	
~ one's nest	das eigene Nest beschmutzen

a founding father	Gründervater
four:	
the ~ corners of the world	abgelegene Regionen
a ~-leaved clover	Glücksklee
~-letter words	Flüche
the fourth estate	die Presse
free:	
a ~ fight	eine Massenschlägerei
a ~ loader	Schnorrer
~ speech	Recht auf freie Meinungsäußerung
make ~ with s.th.	mit etwas umgehen, als gehöre es einem
make ~ with s.b.	sich jdm. gegenüber viel herausnehmen
~ and easily	lässig
~-handed	großzügig
a French letter	Kondom
a fresh start	Neuanfang
fret and fume	Ungeduld oder Angespanntheit zeigen
He spent ages in the bathroom while the rest of the group fretted and fumed.	
A friend in need is a friend indeed. (Sprichw.)	Freunde in der Not gehen tausend auf ein Lot.
frills and furbellows	Firlefanz, überflüssige Dekoration
from:	
~ afar	aus großer Entfernung
~ beginning to end	von Anfang bis Ende
~ the cradle to the grave	von der Wiege bis zur Bahre
~ here to Eternity	für immer
~ log cabin to White House	vom Tellerwäscher zum Millionär
~ pillar to post	von Ort zu Ort

~ bad to worse	vom Regen in die Traufe
~ rags to riches	von Armut zum Reichtum
~ start to finish	von Anfang bis Ende
straight ~ the horse's mouth	direkt von der Quelle
~ the money point of view	unter Berücksichtigung der finanziellen Aspekte
~ time immemorial	seit allen Zeiten
~ the outset	von Anfang an
~ top to bottom	durch die Bank
~ the word go	so bald es möglich war
They have been trying to get into this business from the word go.	

front:

have the ~ to do s.th.	die Stirn haben, etwas zu tun
put on a bold ~	einer Sache tapfer ins Gesicht sehen; tun, als ob man keine Angst hat
When you are afraid of a dog, it's best to just put on a bold front.	

the fruits of one's labour	die Früchte von jds. Arbeit
out of the frying-pan and into the fire	vom Regen in die Traufe

full:

~ of hot air	voller Unsinn, (viel) unnützes Zeug (reden)
~ of beans	glücklich, übermütig
~ frontal	Nacktdarstellung
at ~ length	in voller Länge
~ pelt	mit Höchstgeschwindigkeit
~ steam ahead	mit aller Kraft
at ~ throttle	voller Energie
~ well	sehr wohl (adv.)
He knew full well that he was wrong.	

have fun and games (Sl.)	herumblödeln, Unsinn machen
the fur begins to fly	die Auseinandersetzung geht erst richtig los

It was only when I began to talk back to him that the fur began to fly, but I could not stand it any longer!

furred, four-footed and feathered friends	Tierwelt
fuss:	
~ and bother	unnötige Aufregung
make no ~ about s.th.	nicht viel Aufhebens machen
~ about	Aufhebens machen um

G

the gaiety of nations	allgemeine Erheiterung
gain:	
~ ground	Fortschritte machen, an Boden gewinnen
~ on s.b/s.th.	sich jdm./etwas nähern, jdn. einholen
In the race, the American athlete kept gaining on his English rival.	
gales of laughter	lautes Gelächter
gall and wormwood	eine Sache, an die man sich ungern erinnert
Seeing the pictures of another artist was gall and wormwood to Henry.	
game:	
be ~ for s.th.	bei etwas mitmachen
make ~ of s.b.	auf Kosten von jdm. Spaß haben, jdn. zum Besten halten
The ~'s up.	Das Spiel ist aus.
have the ~ in one's hands	die Sache fest im Griff haben
play the ~	sich an die Spielregeln halten
Cheating is not fair. You must learn to play the game.	
garden gnome	Gartenzwerg
gas up (Am./Sl.)	(auf)tanken
gather:	
~ momentum	an Tempo gewinnen
~ ye rosebuds while ye may	man soll etwas genießen, so lange es möglich ist
run the gauntlet	Spießruten laufen

generation gap	Mangel an Verständnis zwischen Alt und Jung
generous to a fault	übermäßig großzügig, verschwenderisch
a gentleman's agreement	eine formlose, aber bindende Vereinbarung
the genuine article	authentisch
get:	
~ above o.s.	sich überschätzen
You are getting above yourself, you'll never manage that.	
~ ahead	vorankommen, Karriere machen
~ along with s.o.	mit jdm. auskommen
They got along well from the moment they met.	
~ along without s.o./s.th.	ohne jdn./etwas auskommen
~ an airing	offen zum Ausdruck gebracht werden
~ away	1. entwischen, entkommen, 2. wegkommen, in Urlaub gehen
1. The police gave chase but the thief got away. *2. I have worked so hard lately, I must get away for a few days.*	
~ away with you!	Ach, hör doch auf!
~ behind with	in Rückstand geraten mit
I can't take time off to go to the cinema. I'm getting behind with my work.	
~ the bird	rüde oder rücksichtslos abgewiesen werden
~ carried away	sich mitreißen lassen
~ down to business	zur Sache kommen
~ edgeways	seitwärts, von der Seite
~ in touch with	Kontakt aufnehmen mit, anrufen
~ it over and done with	etwas ein und für alle Mal hinter sich bringen
~ one's teeth into s.th.	sich in etwas verbeißen
~ out of hand	außer Kontrolle geraten

We must discuss the situation carefully before it gets out of hand.	
~ out of my way!	Geh mir aus dem Weg!
~ rid of s.th.	etwas loswerden
~ s.th. off one's chest	sich etwas von der Seele reden
Once she had got the whole story off her chest she felt better.	
~ to grips with s.b.	sich mit jdm. auseinandersetzen
~ to know s.th.	etwas in Erfahrung bringen
~ to the bottom of s.th.	einer Sache auf den Grund gehen
The police have never really got to the bottom of that crime.	
~ wind of s.th.	von einer Sache Wind bekommen
If my father gets wind of the plan, he'll forbid it.	
I don't know what got into me.	Ich weiß nicht, was in mich gefahren ist.
It ~s about.	Es spricht sich herum.
Let them ~ on with it.	Lass sie nur so weitermachen.
~ a break	Glück haben
The applicant hoped he would get a break and win the competition.	
~ the chop	entlassen werden
~ a dusty answer	eine enttäuschende oder ablehnende Antwort bekommen
~ a hand	Applaus bekommen
The singer got a good hand at the end of the concert.	
~ a bad name	seinen Ruf ruinieren
~ a move on (Sl.)	von etwas angemacht werden
~ a load off one's mind (Sl.)	etwas loswerden
~ a word in edgeways	zu Wort kommen
Everyone was talking so fast I couldn't get a word in edgeways.	
~ cracking (Sl.)	etwas Dampf machen, loslegen
We'll never finish the job in time if we don't get cracking.	
~ down to brass tacks (Sl.)	Tacheles reden
~ down to the nitty-gritty	zur Sache kommen

~ goose bumps (Am.)/**goose pimples** (Brit.)	eine Gänsehaut bekommen
~ mad	wütend werden
~ mad at s.o.	sich über jdn. ärgern
I got so mad with my daughter, I wanted to slap her.	
~ off scot-free	ungeschoren davonkommen
~ on s.o.'s nerves	jdm. auf die Nerven gehen
~ on with it! (Sl.)	Wach auf! Gib dir einen Ruck!
~ one's act together (Sl.)	Ordnung in die Sache bringen, sich am Riemen reißen
I must get my act together before I present my project to the committee.	
~ one's fingers burned	sich die Finger verbrennen
~ s.th. under one's belt (Sl.)	sich etwas 'reinziehen
I'm so hungry, I'd feel much better if I got a good meal under my belt.	
~ the boot	den Laufpass kriegen
~ the cold shoulder	die kalte Schulter gezeigt bekommen
~ the hang of s.th. (Sl.)	herauskriegen, wie etwas funktioniert
~ the sack (Sl.)	entlassen werden
~ up on the wrong side of the bed	mit dem falschen Fuß aufstehen
~-up-and-go	Energie, Tatkraft, Motivation
Just look at John, he can't wait to start the game. He's full of get-up-and-go.	

ghost:

give up the ~	den Geist aufgeben
not have a ~ of a chance (Sl.)	nicht die geringste Chance haben

gift:

a ~ from the gods	unerwarteter Vorteil, Gottesgeschenk
to have the ~ of the gab	redegewandt sein
don't look a ~ horse in the mouth	einem geschenkten Gaul schaut man nicht ins Maul

gild:	
~ **the lily**	des Guten zu viel tun
~ **the pill**	die bittere Pille versüßen
~ed youth	sorglose Jugendliche
a ginger group	Aktionsgruppe
give:	
~ **the alarm**	Alarm auslösen
~ **s.b. the all-clear**	jdm. Entwarnung geben
~ **as good as one gets**	es jdm. mit gleicher Münze heimzahlen
Peter can take care of himself in an argument. He can give as good as he gets.	
~ **birth to**	zur Welt bringen
~ **cause for**	Grund geben für
~ **chase**	verfolgen
~ **credit where credit is due**	Ehre wem Ehre gebührt
Let's give credit where credit is due, you have written a marvellous book.	
~ **ear to**	anhören
~ **s.o. free rein**	jdm. freie Hand lassen
We gave the au-pair girl free rein with the care of the children.	
~ **in**	aufgeben, nachgeben
~ **it to s.o. straight** (Sl.)	jdm. etwas klar und deutlich sagen
~ **of one's best**	sein Bestes geben
~ **o.s. airs**	sich aufspielen
Don't be so superior, stop giving yourself airs!	
~ **out**	kaputtgehen
My washing-machine has finally given out on me, I must buy a new one.	
~ **rise to s.th.**	etwas verursachen
The bad state of the building gave rise to much criticism.	
~ **s.o. a buzz** (Sl.)	jdn. anrufen
~ **s.o. a dirty look**	jdn. böse anschauen

He gave his father a dirty look when he criticised him.

~ s.o. a hand with s.th. — jdm. bei etwas helfen

Will you give me a hand to move the furniture for the party?

~ s.o. a pain (Sl.) — jdn. ärgern, stören

~ s.o./s.th. away — jdn. verraten, etwas ausplaudern

~ s.o. the glad eyes (Sl.) — jdn. anschmachten

~ s.o. trouble — jdm. Schwierigkeiten machen

~ s.o. the green light — jdm. grünes Licht geben

~ s.o. what for (Sl.) — es jdm. geben

~ s.th. a lick and a promise (Sl.) — etwas oberflächlich tun

Shirley, you should clean your room properly, not just give it a lick and a promise.

~ the game away (Sl.) — einen Plan verraten

~ up the ghost (Sl.) — den Geist aufgeben, sterben

~ up a secret — ein Geheimnis preisgeben

~ way to — Platz machen

glad:

~ tidings — erfreuliche Neuigkeiten

to put one's ~ rags on — sich aufdonnern

glance:

~ at — einen Blick werfen auf

~ over s.th. — etwas überfliegen, den Blick schweifen lassen

He merely glanced over the paper, he didn't have time to read it carefully.

a gleam of hope — ein Hoffnungsschimmer

catch a glimpse of — nur flüchtig zu sehen bekommen

glove:

be hand in ~ with s.o. — mit jdm. unter einer Decke stecken

treat s.o. with kid ~s — jdn. mit Samthandschuhen anfassen

a glutton for work — immer zur Arbeit bereit

Josie is a real glutton for work, you can always find her in the office.

gnashing of teeth	Zähneknirschen
go:	
a ~	ein Versuch
have a ~ (Sl.)	1. versuchen, 2. an die Reihe kommen
1. You can do it if you try, have a go. *2. It's my go to throw the bell.*	
~ a long way	wesentlich zu etwas beitragen
~ all out to do s.th. (Sl.)	alles dransetzen, etwas zu tun
~ about one's business	sich um seine eigenen Angelegenheiten kümmern
~ about s.th.	herangehen an, in Angriff nehmen
~ against the grain	gegen den Strich gehen
It goes very much against the grain to admit that my enemy is right.	
~ ahead!	mach weiter!, nur zu!
~ along with s.o. (Sl.)	mit jdm. übereinstimmen
~ at each other	aufeinander losgehen, streiten
~ back on one's word	ein Versprechen/Wort nicht halten
~ bananas (Am./Sl.)	verrückt werden
~ behind s.o.'s back	jdn. hintergehen
~ beyond one's duty	seine Kompetenz überschreiten
~ by s.o.'s opinion	sich nach jds. Meinung richten
~ by the board	verloren gehen, kaputt gehen
Your plan has gone by the board, the trip has been cancelled.	
~ by the rules	sich an die Regeln halten
~ cold turkey (Am./Sl.)	sofort aufhören, etwas abbrechen
When drug addicts go cold turkey they become very ill.	
~ down fighting	bis zum bitteren Ende kämpfen
~ down in history	in die Geschichte eingehen
The last decade was a time of such tremendous change. I'm sure it will go down in history.	

~ **downhill**	sich rapide verschlechtern, abwärts gehen
He has gone downhill since his wife left him.	
~ **down the drain**	schief gehen
~ **down well with s.o.**	bei jdm. gut ankommen
~ **easy on s.o.**	lieb/vorsichtig mit jdm. sein
~ **fly a kite!** (Am./Sl.)	Hau ab und lass mich in Ruhe.
~ **for s.th.** (Sl.)	sich um etwas bemühen
~ **from bad to worse**	immer schlechter werden
~ **haywire** (Sl.)	durchdrehen
~ **in for s.th.** (Sl.)	sich für etwas interessieren
~ **for nothing**	keine Anerkennung finden
~ **in one ear and out the other**	zum einen Ohr hinein, zum anderen hinaus gehen
~ **like clockwork** (Sl.)	wie am Schnürchen laufen
~ **off the deep end**	überstürzt, den Gefühlen gehorchend handeln
He has gone completely off the deep end with his new girl-friend.	
~ **on and on**	immer weiter machen
~ **on at s.o.**	ständig mit jdm. herumschimpfen, ständig an jdm. herumnörgeln
~ **one better**	es besser machen
~ **places** (Sl.)	eine Zukunft haben
Cecilia is a very talented actress, she will obviously go places.	
~ **sky high** (Sl.)	ins Unermessliche steigen, sehr hoch hinaufgehen
Everything is so expensive these days, prices have gone sky high.	
~ **through thick and thin**	durch dick und dünn gehen
My friend and I were inseparable at school, we went through thick and thin together.	
~ **through the roof**	vor Wut an die Decke gehen
John got so angry with his dog he almost went through the roof.	
~ **to great lengths**	sein Möglichstes tun
~ **to pieces**	1. kaputt gehen, zu Bruch gehen, 2. zusammenbrechen
1. My ball-dress is so old it is going to pieces.	

2. When she heard of his death she went to pieces.	
~ to the dogs	vor die Hunde gehen
~ to town (Sl.)	1. hart/schnell arbeiten, 2. übertrieben viel Geld ausgeben
1. Just look how fast they are working, they really are going to town.	
2. They really went to town about entertaining their friends.	
it's no ~ (Sl.)	nichts zu machen
That just goes to show that ...	Das beweist nur, dass ...
That goes without saying.	Das versteht sich von selbst.
to be on the ~ (Sl.)	ständig unterwegs

God:

~ damn	Verdammt!
~ damn s.b.'s eyes	jmd. soll verdammt sein
~ forbid	da sei der Himmel vor
~ helps those who help themselves. (Sprichw.)	Hilf dir selbst, dann hilft dir Gott!
~ moves in a mysterious way (his wonders to perform). (Sprichw.)	Die Wege des Herrn sind unergründlich.

going:

a ~ concern	ein florierendes Geschäft
~, ~, gone	Zum ersten, zum zweiten, zum dritten!
the ~ rate	der übliche Preis
still ~ strong	nach wie vor aktiv oder erfolgreich
a gold mine	eine Goldmine

golden:

a ~ handshake	Geschenk zum Ruhestand
a ~ opportunity	eine hervorragende Gelegenheit
a ~ rule	eine goldene Regel

good:

the ~ book	Bibel
a ~ deal of	eine Menge
one's ~ deed for the day	die gute Tat des Tages

as ~ as it gets *I know everything is far from perfect, but I'm afraid this is as good as it gets.*	besser wird's nicht
~ for a laugh	erheiternd
It's no ~ crying.	Es nützt nichts, wenn du weinst.
~ for nothing	Tunichtgut, Taugenichts; zu nichts nütze
~ and proper	gründlich
~ gracious!	Du meine Güte!
~ riddance	Gut, dass wir das los sind!
for ~	für immer
~s and chattels	Besitztümer
My goose is cooked. (Sl.)	Das Ding ist gelaufen.
one's gorge rises	Ekel oder Übelkeit fühlen
grace and favour	guter Wille (im Gegensatz zu Verpflichtungen)
gracious living	Luxusleben
the grand manner	großartiges Auftreten
grasp the nettle	resolut mit einer Schwierigkeit umgehen
grass:	
The ~ is always greener on the other side. (Sprichw.)	Die Kirschen in Nachbars Garten sind süßer. Man hält immer das für besser, was man nicht hat.
~ widow	Strohwitwe
grease s.b.'s palms	jdn. schmieren, bestechen
Greek:	
It's all ~ to me.	Für mich sind das böhmische Dörfer.
The ~s had a name for it.	Etwas gibt es schon seit langer Zeit.

green:	
go ~ with envy (Sl.)	gelb vor Neid
have ~ fingers	einen grünen Daumen haben
see any green in s.o.'s eye	jdn. für einen Dummkopf halten
grey:	
a ~ eminence	eine graue Eminenz, jmd., der im Hintergrund die Fäden in der Hand hält
~ matter	Gehirn, Intelligenz
grin:	
~ like a Cheshire cat	wie ein Honigkuchenpferd grinsen
~ and bear it (Sl.)	in den sauren Apfel beißen
grind one's teeth	mit den Zähnen knirschen
grip:	
come to ~s with s.th.	etwas anpacken
take a ~ on oneself (Sl.)	sich zusammenreißen, sich einen Ruck geben
grist for s.b.'s mill	Wasser auf jds. Mühle
grit one's teeth *The only way to face something unpleasant is to grit one's teeth and bear it.*	die Zähne zusammenbeißen
ground:	
~ed (Sl.)	Stubenarrest haben
be dashed to the ~	am Boden zerstört sein
be well ~ed in *There's no doubt he'll pass the examination, he's so well-grounded in all the subjects.*	bewandert sein in
gain ~	an Boden gewinnen
have one's feet on the ~	mit beiden Beinen fest auf der Erde stehen
lose ~	an Boden verlieren
stay one's ~	sich behaupten

grow:	
~ in strength	stärker werden
~ out of s.th.	1. aus etwas herauswachsen, 2. zu alt für etwas werden
1. John has grown out of his shoes yet again. 2. I'm twenty now and have grown out of such childish things.	
~ old gracefully	würdevoll altern
~ on s.o. (Sl.)	mit der Zeit ans Herz wachsen
to bear s.o. a grudge	jdm. böse sein
guard:	
~ against	sich hüten vor
on one's ~	auf der Hut; vorbereitet
Be on your guard, they may still come and catch you.	
guardian angel	Schutzengel
guiding light	leuchtendes Vorbild
guinea-pig	Versuchskaninchen
gun:	
~ for s.o. (Sl.)	jdn. suchen, um ihm zu schaden/strafen
The headmaster is gunning for you, he knows you missed the cricket match.	
a big ~ (Sl.)	ein wichtiger, einflussreicher Mensch
George is one of the big guns in his profession.	
stick to one's ~s	seinen Standpunkt fest behaupten
the gutter press	Sensationspresse

H

habit:

break a ~	sich etwas abgewöhnen
kick the ~ (Sl.)	abgewöhnen, aufgeben
make a ~ of s.th.	sich etwas zur Gewohnheit machen

hail:

within ~	in Rufweite
~ from	ursprünglich herstammen/kommen

McGregor hails from Scotland. I'm from New York. Where do you hail from?

hair:

keep one's ~ on	sich beherrschen
a ~ of the dog that bit you (Sl.)	ein Schluck Alkohol gegen den Kater

There's only one cure for a hangover and that is some of the hair of the dog that bit you.

let one's ~ down (Sl.)	aus sich herausgehen
split ~s	über unwichtige, banale Sachen streiten, Haarspaltereien betreiben
My ~'s standing on end.	Die Haare stehen mir zu Berge.

I was so afraid my hair stood on end.

hale and hearty	gesund

half:

~-baked	noch grün hinter den Ohren
by ~	Ausdruck der Übertreibung

You must have a serious talk with John, he is too cheeky by half.

~ cut	angetrunken
~ seas over (Brit./Sl.)	betrunken
that's ~ the battle	damit ist viel gewonnen

too ... by ~	viel zu ...
~ a loaf is better than no bread. (Sprichw.)	Der Spatz in der Hand ist besser als die Taube auf dem Dach.
~ a mo (Sl.)	Moment!
do things by halves	halbe Sachen machen

hammer:

~ at s.th.	eifrig an etwas arbeiten
~ s.th. into s.b. *It took the teacher all morning to hammer the theory into his pupils.*	jdm. etwas einbläuen
~ and tongs *He may not be any good as a pianist but he certainly goes at it hammer and tongs.*	mit viel Lärm/Kraft/ Enthusiasmus
~ out (Brit./Sl.) *We spent all weekend hammering out our plans for the future.*	nach vielen Diskussionen zu einer Entscheidung kommen

a halfway house	Kompromiss
the hall of fame	die Ruhmeshalle

hand:

an old ~ *Let me help. I'm an old hand at mending things.*	ein Mensch mit viel Erfahrung
at first ~	aus erster Hand
change ~s *This house has changed hands many times.*	den Besitzer wechseln
gain the upper ~	gewinnen
do s.th. off ~	etwas aus dem Stegreif tun, etwas nebenbei tun
~ down to	vererben, weitergeben an
lend a ~	helfen
on the other ~	andererseits
~ in glove with s.o. *The doctor and his nursing staff really work hand in glove.*	sehr eng, nahe
out of ~	außer Kontrolle

~-me-down	ein weitergereichtes Kleidungsstück
Why can't I have a new dress? I hate always wearing hand-me-downs.	
~ over fist	sehr schnell
What a good day we've had at the flea market. We took in money hand over fist.	
~ s.th. in	abgeben
have a ~ in s.th.	teilhaben an, die Finger in einer Angelegenheit haben
John knows all about the scheme. He must have had a hand in the planning.	
lay ~s on s.th.	etwas in die Finger bekommen
throw in one's ~	aufgeben
turn one's ~ to s.th. (Sl.)	sich einer Sache oder Tätigkeit zuwenden
wash one's ~s of s.th.	nichts mit einer Sache zu tun haben wollen
you have got to ~ to s.o. (Sl.)	das muss man jemandem lassen
handle with kid gloves	mit Samthandschuhen anfassen
hang:	
~ about	herumlungern
~ around	bleiben
~ back	zögern, sich sträuben
~ by a single thread	am seidenen Faden hängen
~ in the balance	unentschlossen sein
The whole issue will just have to hang in the balance until father returns.	
~ one's head	den Kopt hängen lassen
~ on!	Halt! Moment!
~ on s.b.'s lips/words	an jds. Lippen hängen
The child was fascinated by the story his grandmother was telling and hung on to her every word.	
~ out (Sl.)	1. hausen, sich aufhalten, 2. verkehren mit

1. I hang out in the East End of London.	
2. I'm afraid Mary might be hanging out with the wrong people.	
~ up	den Telefonhörer auflegen

happen:

~ on s.b.	zufällig auf jdn. treffen
I walked into the library and happened on John and David.	
~ what may! (Brit.)	Was auch immer geschieht!

happy:

a ~ coincindence	ein glückliches Zusammentreffen von Ereignissen
the ~ couple	ein frisch verheiratetes Paar
a ~ hunting ground	Paradies

hard:

~ by	in der Nähe von
be ~ one s.b.	jdm. schwer zusetzen
~ to come by	schwer zu bekommen
a ~ nut to crack	eine harte Nuss zu knacken
~ on s.o.'s heels	dicht hinterher
~ put to do s.th.	etwas mit Schwierigkeiten tun
~-to-get	sich zieren
~ up (Sl.)	blank, ohne Kohle
~ and fast	1. festgelegt, präzise, 2. mit Energie
1. There are no hard and fast rules for these occasions, you just have to decide on the spot.	
2. He played the game hard and fast, but it was great fun.	
~ of hearing	schwerhörig

hare:

~-brained	dumm, unverantwortlich
run with the ~ and hunt with the hounds (Sl.)	auf zwei Hochzeiten tanzen

be out of harm's way	außer Gefahr sein, keinen Unfug anrichten können

make a hash of s.th.	Chaos anrichten, etwas in den Sand setzen
Make haste!	Beeile dich!
hat:	
at the drop of a ~	ohne Weiteres
eat one's ~	einen Besen fressen
hatch a plot	einen Plan entwerfen
bury the hatchet	das Kriegsbeil begraben
hate:	
~ s.b.'s guts	jdn. verabscheuen
~ the sight of s.b.	den Anblick von jdm. nicht ertragen können
haul s.o. over the coals	jdn. zur Schnecke machen
have:	
~ a bone to pick with s.b.	mit jdm. ein Hühnchen zu rupfen haben
~ a brush with s.th.	mit etwas kurz in Kontakt/ Berührung kommen
When I had pneumonia as a child I had a brush with death, but I got over it.	
~ a close shave	glimpflich davonkommen
~ a fit (Sl.)	einen Wutanfall bekommen
~ a fling with s.o.	mit jdm. eine Affäre haben
~ a go at s.th.	etwas versuchen
~ a good command of s.th.	etwas beherrschen/gut können
He has a good command of English.	
~ a good head on one's shoulders	ein kluger Kopf sein, intelligent sein
~ a hand in s.th.	die Hand im Spiel haben
~ a hold over s.b.	jdn. in der Hand haben
~ a lot on one's mind	viel im Kopf haben
I'm sorry I forgot to write you. I've had a lot on my mind recently.	

~ a mind to	Lust haben zu
~ a near miss	knapp (mit dem Leben) davonkommen
~ a say in s.th.	mitreden, etwas zu sagen haben
~ a screw loose (Sl.)	eine Schraube locker haben
~ a sweet tooth	gern Süßes essen
Jane loves ice cream. She has a sweet tooth.	
~ a swelled head (Am/Sl.)	eingebildet sein
~ a whale of a time (Sl.)	sehr viel Spaß haben
~ a word with s.o.	mit jdm. ein Wörtchen reden
~ ants in one's pants	unruhig sein, rastlos sein
~ bats in one's belfry (Sl.)	nicht alle Tassen im Schrank haben
~ had it (Sl.)	erledigt sein, am Ende sein, ausgespielt haben
~ had one's fill	gesättigt sein
~ it in for s.o. (Sl.)	es auf jdn. abgesehen haben
~ it out with s.o.	ausdiskutieren
~ one's feet on the ground	mit beiden Beinen auf dem Boden stehen
~ one's finger in the pie	mitmischen
~ one's head in the clouds	geistesabwesend sein
~ one's heart in one's mouth	sein Herz auf der Zunge tragen
~ one's nose in the air	hochnäsig sein
~ one's way	es machen, wie man will; sich durchsetzen
~ one's wits about one	alle seine Sinne beieinander haben
You have to have your wits about you when driving a car.	
~ a row with s.o.	Streit mit jdm. haben
~ second thoughts	Zweifel bekommen
~ s.th. up one's sleeve	ein Geheimnis/eine Überraschung parat haben
~ s.th. wrapped up	etwas erklärt/erledigt haben
~ the courage of one's convictions	Zivilcourage haben
~ the gift of the gab (Sl.)	gut im Reden sein, überzeugend sein
~ the guts to do s.th. (Sl.)	den Mumm haben, etwas zu tun
~ the time of one's life	einen Mordsspaß haben

~ too many irons in the fire	zu viele Eisen im Feuer haben, zu viel auf einmal anpacken
~ what it takes	das gewisse Etwas haben
Make hay while the sun shines. (Sprichw.)	das Eisen schmieden, solange es heiß ist
to go haywire (Sl.)	durchdrehen
head:	
be off one's ~ (Sl.)	verrückt sein
not make ~ or tail of s.th.	sich keinen Reim auf etwas machen können, aus etwas nicht klug werden
I can't make head or tail of what she's saying.	
have a good ~ on one's shoulders	ein kluger Kopf sein
keep one's ~	einen kühlen Kopf bewahren
keep one's ~ above water	sich über Wasser halten können
be ~ over heels in love	bis über beide Ohren verliebt sein
talk one's ~ off	sich dumm und dusselig reden
talk over one's ~	jdn. sprachlich überfordern
take the ~	die Führung übernehmen
run ~ over heels	Hals über Kopf davonstürzen
~ and shoulders above	weit voraus/überlegen sein
have one's ~ screwed on the right way	intelligent/klug sein
John will make the right decision. He has his head screwed on the right way.	
~ on	frontal
The two trains collided head on.	
to be a headache (Sl.)	jdn. nerven
hear:	
~ the last of s.b.	mit jdm. fertig sein
~ s.o. out	jdn. ausreden lassen
in my ~ing	in meiner Gegenwart
~ from s.o.	eine Botschaft/einen Brief von jdm. bekommen

heart:	
~ to ~	im Vertrauen, zwischen Freunden
after one's own ~	nach dem eigenem Geschmack
break s.o.'s ~	jdm. das Herz brechen
find it in one's ~ to	es übers Herz bringen
I could not find it in my heart to tell him.	
have a ~	sei so nett
have one's ~ in one's boots (Sl.)	sehr deprimiert sein, Angst haben
have one's ~ in one's mouth	erschrocken sein
have the ~ to do s.th.	etwas übers Herz bringen
learn s.th. by ~	etwas auswendig lernen
lose ~	den Mut verlieren
It is very easy to lose heart when nothing goes right.	
lose one's ~ to s.o.	sein Herz an jdn. verlieren
take s.th. to ~	sich etwas zu Herzen nehmen
wear one's ~ on one's sleeves	aus seinem Herzen keine Mördergrube machen
hearth and home	Heim und Herd
in the heat of the moment	im Eifer des Gefechts
heaven:	
~ on earth	ein himmlischer Ort
the ~s open	es regnet
heavy:	
the ~ father	ein autoritärer Vater
~ going	eine schwierige oder mühsame Tätigkeit
Loading the car turned out to be heavy going.	
heel:	
dig one's ~s in	sich stur stellen
take to one's ~s	die Beine in die Hand nehmen, ausreißen
When I saw the bull in the field, I look to my heels and fled.	

kick one's ~s	Zeit verschwenden/vertrödeln
the height of folly	der Höhepunkt der Dummheit
hell:	
~-bent on doing s.th.	wild entschlossen, etwas zu tun
all ~ breaks loose	der Teufel ist los
~ for leather	mit größtmöglichem Tempo
help:	
~ a lame dog over a stile	jdm. helfen, der in Schwierigkeiten steckt, jdm. in der Not beistehen
~ o.s. to s.th.	sich etwas nehmen, sich bedienen
~ s.b. with s.th.	jdm. bei etwas behilflich sein
here:	
~ below	in diesem Leben
~ goes!	Jetzt geht's los!
~ and now	jetzt und hier
~ and there	an verschiedenen Orten
~, there and everywhere	an den unterschiedlichsten Orten, überall
~ today and gone tomorrow	heute hier, morgen vergangen
~'s to …	Toast auf …
Here's to Louise who is celebrating her birthday tonight!	
hey presto	Abrakadabra! (Zauberwort)
the hidden persuaders	die Werbebranche
high:	
be in ~ spirits	gute Laune haben
~ and dry	verlassen
~-handed	arrogant
~ jinks	Blödsinn, Scherze
~ and low	überall
~ and mighty	arrogant
~ summer	Hochsommer
~, wide and handsome	beeindruckend, optisch ansprechend

The ~er you climb the harder you fall. (Sprichw.)	Wer hoch steigt kann tief fallen.
fly ~	ehrgeizig sein
It's ~ time.	Es ist höchste Zeit.
Goodness, it's past ten o'clock. It's high time we went home.	
hint:	
drop a ~	einen dezenten Hinweis geben
give a broad ~	einen Wink mit dem Zaunpfahl geben
take a ~	einen Wink verstehen
hit:	
~-and-miss	unüberlegt, ziellos
~ at s.th.	nach etwas schlagen
~ back	zurückschlagen
~ bottom (Sl.)	einen Tiefpunkt erreichen
~ on	stoßen auf
~ or miss	auf gut Glück
~ it off with s.o.	mit jdm. schnell warm werden
As I have the same interests as Jane, we hit it off immediately.	
~ s.o. below the belt	jdn. unter der Gürtellinie treffen
~ the ceiling (Sl.)	in die Luft gehen (vor Wut)
~ the sack (Sl.)	sich aufs Ohr hauen, ins Bett gehen
~ the nail on the head	den Nagel auf den Kopf treffen
~ the roof	an die Decke gehen
hither and thither	ziellos von einem Ort zum anderen
They moved hither and thither for a few years before finally settling down in the city.	
to hog s.th. (Sl.)	etwas an sich reißen
hold:	
have a ~ of s.th.	etwas beherrschen
~ in high regard	hoch achten, in Ehren halten
~ all the aces (Sl.)	alle Asse in der Hand halten, eine gute Ausgangsposition haben

Don't ~ your breath.	Warte gar nicht erst darauf, dass es passiert!
~ forth	lang reden
Janet is incredibly boring. She can hold forth for ages on the most uninteresting subjects.	
~ good	gültig sein
~ one's own	sich behaupten
A shy person always has difficulty holding his own in an argument.	
~ one's peace	sich nicht einmischen, still/ruhig bleiben
~ one's tongue	nicht sprechen, den Mund halten
~ out	aushalten
He has lost a lot of blood in the car crash, I hope he can hold out till the ambulance gets here.	
~ the line!	Bleiben Sie bitte am Apparat!
~ true	sich bewahrheiten
keep ~ of s.th.	etwas festhalten
take ~ of s.th.	Besitz ergreifen von
~ water	stimmen, überzeugen
~ with s.th.	einverstanden sein

hole:

a ~ and corner business	eine zwielichtige Tätigkeit
a ~ in the wall	ein sehr kleiner Laden
be in a ~ (Sl.)	in der Klemme sitzen

holier than thou	selbstgerecht

hollow:

a ~ laugh	ein gezwungenes Lachen
to beat s.o. hollow	jdn. überlegen schlagen

holy:

~ war	heiliger Krieg
a ~ terror	eine furchteinflößende Person

home:

a ~ bird	ein Stubenhocker
drive s.th. ~ to s.b.	jdm. etwas klarmachen

It took me a long time to drive the point home to him, but I think he understood in the end.

hit ~	ins Schwarze treffen
make o.s. at ~	es sich bequem machen

Homer sometimes nods. (Sprichw.)	Irren ist menschlich.

honest to God	Ehrlich!

Honesty is the best policy. (Sprichw.)	Ehrlich währt am längsten.

honour:

a debt of ~	Ehrenschulden
a point of ~	Ehrensache
~ among thieves	Ganovenehre

hook:

on one's own ~	auf eigene Faust
by ~ or by crook	auf Biegen und Brechen
~, line and sinker	ganz und gar, komplett
off the ~	aus der Klemme

He's really to blame for getting himself into this situation, but we must see if we can get him off the hook.

play ~y (Am./Sl.)	Schule schwänzen
~ed on s.th. (Sl.)	einer Sache (Droge) verfallen sein, süchtig sein

Nobody cares two hoots about it.	Danach kräht kein Hahn.

hop:

keep s.b. on the hop	jdn. in Ruhe lassen
be ~ping mad (Sl.)	stinksauer sein
~ to it! (Sl.)	Beweg' dich! Mach schnell!

stir up a hornet's nest	in ein Wespennest stechen

horse:

back the wrong ~	auf das falsche Pferd setzen
have ~ sense	einen gesunden Menschenverstand haben
sit on a high ~	auf einem hohen Ross sitzen
straight from the ~'s mouth	direkt von der Quelle, aus erster Hand
~ play (Sl.)	das Herumtoben
Reckon without one's host.	Die Rechnung ohne den Wirt machen.

hot:

a ~ spot	Brennpunkt
get into ~ water (Sl.)	in Teufels Küche kommen
go like ~ cakes	weggehen wie warme Semmeln
talk a lot of ~ air (Sl.)	Blödsinn reden
~ and bothered *The witness grew hot and bothered when the judge asked him a question.*	aufgeregt, ängstlich
~ under the collar	wütend, verlegen, durcheinander

house:

~ of cards	Kartenhaus, instabile Konstruktion
bring down the ~	hervorragend spielen (Theater)
keep (an) open ~	ein offenes Haus haben, Leute zu jeder Zeit willkommen heißen
like a ~ on fire *She was working away like a house on fire.*	schnell, mit Elan
put one's ~ in order	vor seiner eigenen Tür kehren
it's a household name	das ist ein Begriff

how:

~ about ...?	Wie wär's mit ...?
~ are things?	Wie geht's?
~ come?	Wieso das?
~ crazy can you get?	Gibt es keine Grenzen der Verrücktheit?

~ dare s.b.	wie kann es jmd. wagen
~ on earth	wie zur Hölle
~'s the world been treating you?	Wie ist es dir ergangen?
hug o.s. about s.th.	sich selbst zu etwas beglückwünschen/gratulieren
howl:	
a ~ of protest	ein Aufschrei der Entrüstung
a ~ing success	ein herausragender Erfolg
a ~ing wilderness	tiefe Wildnis
a hue and cry	Alarm, allgemeine Aufregung
humanly possible	menschenmöglich
have the hump	schlechte Laune haben
Hunger is the best sauce. (Sprichw.)	Hunger ist der beste Koch.
hunt:	
~ for/up	suchen
~ after s.th.	etwas nachjagen
~ s.b. down	jdn. zur Strecke bringen
hurt:	
~ s.b.'s feelings	jds. Gefühle verletzen
~ s.b.'s pride	jdn. kränken
hurry:	
be in a ~	in Eile sein, es eilig haben
~ over s.th.	etwas hastig tun/erledigen
~ up!	Beeile dich!
hustle and bustle	geschäftiges Treiben

I

I:	
~ ask you?	Hast Du so etwas schon einmal gehört?
~ beg to differ	ich bin leider anderer Ansicht
~'ll bet!	Ich glaube kein Wort!
~ can tell you!	(bekräftigend:) aber wie!
~ dare say ...	mir scheint sicher, dass ...
~ don't know what the world is coming to.	(oft iron.) Wo soll das noch hinführen!
~ don't mind if ~ do	Danke, herzlich gerne!
Cigarette? – I don't mind if I do!	
~ don't think	das bezweifele ich
~'ll eat my hat	ich fresse einen Besen
~ like that	Von wegen!
~ might add	ich sollte noch darauf hinweisen
~ should think so	Aber sicher!
~'ve had it.	Ich bekomme eins auf den Deckel. Dann kann ich's vergessen. Es ist um mich geschehen.
~ would if ~ could but ~ can't	ich würde ja gerne, aber es geht nicht
~ wouldn't touch it with a barge pole.	Das würde ich nicht mit der Kneifzange anfassen.
ice:	
keep s.th. on ~	eine Sache auf Eis legen
idea:	
the very ~	was für eine lächerliche Vorstellung
form an ~ of s.th.	sich von etwas eine Vorstellung machen
put ~s into s.o.'s head	jdm. Flausen in den Kopf setzen
What's the big ~?	Was soll das? Was hast du für einen Unsinn vor?
if:	
~ any	wenn etwas da sein sollte

~ at all — wenn überhaupt

~ one believes that, one will believe anything — wer so dumm ist, diese Sache zu glauben, beweist damit seinen Mangel an Urteilsvermögen

~ the cap fits, wear it — Wen's juckt, der kratze sich. Man soll sich ruhig angesprochen fühlen, wenn die Kritik zutrifft.

~ need be — falls es wirklich nötig sein sollte

~ the worst comes to the worst ... — Wenn alle Stricke reißen, ... Wenn wirklich alles schief läuft, ...

~ you ask me — wenn du meine Meinung wissen willst

~ you can't beat them, join them — wen man nicht besiegen kann, mit dem muss man sich verbünden

~ you please — wenn du so freundlich wärst

~s and buts — zahlreiche Einwände und Vorbehalte, Wenn und Aber

ill:

~ at ease — unwohl (in der Haut), ängstlich, nervös

A person will often feel ill at ease before an interview.

~-assorted — inkompatibel, schlecht zueinander passend

It's an ~ bird that fouls its own nest. (Sprichw.) — Das eigene Nest beschmutzt man nicht.

~ weeds grow apace. (Sprichw.) — Unkraut vergeht nicht.

impose:

~ on s.b. — jdm. zur Last fallen

~ o.s. on s.b. — sich jdm. aufdrängen

improve:

~ the occasion — eine gegebene Situation zu seinem Vorteil nutzen

~ on s.th. — etwas besser machen

in:

~ a bad way — in schlechter Verfassung

~ a flash (Sl.) — schnell, sofort

~ a fog	geistesabwesend, unachtsam
~ a huff	eingeschnappt
~ a lather (Sl.)	aufgeregt, durcheinander, erhitzt
~ a month of Sundays	ewig lang
I haven't seen you in a month of Sundays, you look well.	
~ a nutshell	knapp ausgedrückt, kurz gefasst
~ a quandary	konfus, durcheinander
~ a light spot	in Schwierigkeiten
~ a vicious circle	in einem Teufelskreis
~ apple-pie order (Am./Sl.)	in guter Verfassung, ordentlich
~ bad taste	geschmacklos
To laugh at a funeral is in very bad taste.	
~ black and white	schriftlich, schwarz auf weiß
~ brief	ganz kurz
~ broad daylight	am helllichten Tag
~ cold blood (Sl.)	grausam, kaltblütig
~ confidence	im Vertrauen gesagt
~ deep (Am./Sl.)	in größten Schwierigkeiten, verschuldet
~ due course	zur richtigen Zeit, mit der Zeit
~ fine feather	gut gelaunt
~ full swing	voll im Gange
The party was in full swing when I arrived.	
~ for a penny, ~ for a pound. (Brit./Sl.)	Wer A sagt, muss auch B sagen.
~ for it (Sl.)	vor Schwierigkeiten stehen
When I saw how angry my father was, I knew I was in for it.	
~ for s.th. (Sl.)	etwas zu erwarten haben
~ good time	schnell, in kurzer Zeit
~ hot water (Sl.)	in Schwierigkeiten
~ less than no time	im Nu
~ no time (at all)	sehr schnell
~ one ear and out the other	zum einen Ohr hinein, zum anderen hinaus
~ one's cups	betrunken
He is likely to start a fight when he's in his cups.	

~ one's mind's eye	vor dem inneren Auge
~ one's right mind	rational, geistig gesund
No one in their right mind would walk into a cage full of lions.	
~ one's Sunday best	im Sonntagskleid/-staat
~ short supply	rar
~ the absence of ...	angesichts der Tatsache, dass etwas oder jmd. fehlt
~ the bag (Sl.)	gewiss, sicher
I've got the contract in the bag, nothing can stop me now.	
~ the doghouse (Sl.)	in Schwierigkeiten
~ the long run	auf lange Sicht, endlich, zum Schluss
~ the middle of nowhere	dort, wo sich Fuchs und Hase „Gute Nacht" sagen
We can't go and see Ann very often, she lives in the middle of nowhere.	
~ the near future	in naher Zukunft
~ the prime of life	im besten Alter
~ the twinkling of an eye	im Nu, im Handumdrehen
My aunt is an excellent cook. She can put a delicious meal on the table in the twinkling of an eye.	
~ this day and age	heutzutage
~-laws	die angeheirateten Verwandten
~s-and-outs	alle Einzelheiten
industrial action	Streik
inside every fat man there is a thin man trying to get out	dicke Menschen haben das Gefühl, dass sie von der Welt falsch eingeschätzt werden
an interested party	diejenigen, die von einer Entwicklung profitieren
into the bargain	zusätzlich
iron:	
the ~ enters one's soul	jmd. wird verbittert
an ~ fist in a velvet glove	ein Wolf im Schafspelz

~ rations	die eiserne Reserve
strike while the ~ is hot	das Eisen schmieden, solange es heiß ist
have too many ~s in the fire	zu viele Eisen im Feuer haben, zu viel auf einmal anpacken
~ s.th./things out	ein Problem ausbügeln

it:

~ never rains but ~ pours. (Sprichw.)	Ein Unglück kommt selten allein.
~'s high time.	Es ist höchste Zeit.
~ beats me (Sl.)	ich komme mit etwas nicht klar
~ can't happen here	so etwas wird hier (oder uns) nie geschehen
~ figures ...	es erscheint vernünftig oder wahrscheinlich, dass ...
~ is all in a day's work	eine Aufgabe, an die man gewöhnt ist, macht einem nichts aus
~ is just as well ... *It was just as well we did not go out that night, as the weather took a turn for the worse.*	es ist ein Glück, dass ...
~ happens that ...	es trifft zufällig zu, dass ...
~ takes two to do s.th.	manche Dinge schafft man nicht alleine
It takes two to tango.	Es gehören immer zwei dazu.
~'s the thought that counts. (Sprichw.)	Der gute Wille zählt.
~'s a small world	wie klein die Welt ist
~'s all in the mind	das ist alles Einbildung
an ivory tower	ein Elfenbeinturm, abgeschottet von der wirklichen Welt
the Ivy league	die Gruppe der älteren und prestigeträchtigen amerikanischen Universitäten

J

Jack:

~ of all trades (and master of none)	ein Hansdampf in allen Gassen
~ is as good as his master.	Wie der Herr, so's G'schärr.
before you can say ~ Robinson	schneller, als du denken kannst

jack:

~ up s.o. (Am./Sl.)	jdn. motivieren
I guess I'll have to jack up the workmen to do the job properly.	
~ up s.th.	1. etwas mittels eines Hebers anheben, 2. Preis anheben
1. The mechanic jacked up the car to look underneath. *2. The telephone company jacked up the price of a call.*	

to hit the jackpot	das große Los ziehen

jam:

~ tomorrow	der Glaube daran, dass sich die Lage bessern wird
~ the brakes on	eine Vollbremsung machen
be in a ~	in der Patsche sitzen

with a jaundiced eye	etwas zynisch betrachten
one's jaw drops	jdm. fällt die Klappe runter
John's jaw dropped when he saw the mess the dog had made.	
jazz s.th. up (Sl.)	etwas aufpeppen, aufregend machen
Most classrooms could do with being jazzed up a bit.	
back in a jiffy (Sl.)	gleich wieder da
the jig is up	alle Hoffnung ist dahin

job:	
the ~ in hand	die Aufgabe, mit der man im Moment beschäftigt ist
a ~ lot	Warenposten
a ~ of work	eine schwierige oder unmögliche Aufgabe
be on the ~	bei der Arbeit sein
It's quite a ~.	Es ist keine einfache Sache. Das ist nicht einfach.
make a good ~ of s.th.	gute Arbeit leisten, etwas ordentlich tun
It isn't my ~.	Das ist nicht mein Bier. Das geht mich nichts an.
a Job's comforter	jmd., der durch seinen Trost die Situation nur verschlimmert
jog:	
~ along	dahintrotten, weiterwursteln
How's life? Jogging along as usual?	
~ s.b.'s arm/elbow	jdn. anstoßen, um seine Aufmerksamkeit zu erregen
~ s.o.'s memory	jdm. auf die Sprünge helfen (geistig)
John Bull	Personifizierung Englands
Johnny-come-lately	jmd., der sich einer Gruppe erst vor kurzem angeschlossen hat, und noch nicht wirklich dazu gehört
join:	
~ hands with	sich die Hände reichen
~ up with s.o.	sich jdm. anschließen
~ forces with s.o.	seine Kräfte mit denen einer anderen Person/Gruppe vereinigen
~ the fray	sich an einer Auseinandersetzung beteiligen
care to ~ s.o.	sich jdm. anschließen
put s.o.'s nose out of joint (Sl.)	jdn. vor den Kopf stoßen, kränken

jolly:

a ~ good s.th. *That was a jolly good movie we saw last week.*	sehr gut
~ well	mit Sicherheit

jot:

~ down	notieren
~ or tittle	das kleinste Detail

journey's end	Tod

joy:

No ~!	Tote Hose
Any ~?	Erfolg gehabt?

a judgement of Solomon	eine weise Entscheidung
stew in one's own juices	im eigenen Saft schmoren lassen

jump:

~ all over s.o. (Am./Sl.)	jdn. wüst beschimpfen, jdn. zur Schnecke machen
~ at s.th.	sich auf etwas stürzen
~ the gun	vorzeitig mit etwas anfangen
~ the queue	sich vordrängeln
~ to one's feet	aufspringen
~ to conclusions	voreilige Schlüsse ziehen, vorschnell urteilen
~ down s.o.'s throat	jdm. über den Mund fahren
~ out of the frying pan into the fire. (Sprichw.)	Vom Regen in die Traufe kommen.
It's the high ~ for s.o.	jmd. kann sich auf etwas gefasst machen

just:

~ another s.th.	nur ein weiteres ... ohne besondere Merkmale
~ anybody	jeder Beliebige
~ as one is	unverändert
~ as soon do s.th. *I'd just as soon go to England for my holiday.*	etwas genauso gut/gerne tun
~ as you like	ganz wie du willst

~ for the ride	nur zum Spaß
~ in case	nur für den Fall
~ like that	einfach so
~ one of those things	eine dieser unvermeidlichen Sachen
~ the job	genau das, was man braucht
~ what the doctor ordered	genau das Richtige
but ~	eben erst
my ~ right	mein volles Recht

K

keen:	
~ on doing s.th.	sehr für etwas sein
~ on s.th.	schätzen, gerne tun
~ on s.o.	für jdn. schwärmen
keep:	
~ a civil tongue in one's head	höflich reden/bleiben
~ a close watch on s.b.	jdn. scharf beobachten
~ a stiff upper lip	kühl, unbewegt bleiben
~ abreast of	mithalten
We do what we can to keep abreast of scientific development.	
~ after s.b.	jdn. verfolgen, jdm. nachstellen
~ an eye on s.o.	jdn. im Auge behalten
~ s.o. at arm's length	sich jdn. vom Leib halten
~ s.th/s.o. at bay	etwas/jdn. abwehren, fern halten
The soldier managed to keep the enemy at bay.	
~ at 1. s.o/2. s.th.	1. herumnörgeln. 2. bei etwas bleiben, festhalten an, darauf bestehen
1. My mother keeps at me to go to university. *2. You'll never learn to play the piano unless you keep at it.*	
~ coming back to s.th.	auf etwas beharren
~ company	verkehren mit
A person is always judged by the company he keeps.	
~ close	wenig sprechen
~ dark	geheim halten
I'm leaving the firm next week, but please keep it dark.	
~ going	dabei bleiben, weitermachen
~ one's fingers crossed	die Daumen drücken
~ in check	in Schranken halten, zügeln
~ in mind	etwas nicht vergessen, an etwas denken
~ in ignorance	in Unkenntnis lassen

~ **in sight**	im Auge behalten
~ **in touch with**	in Kontakt bleiben mit
~ **late hours**	lange aufbleiben, spät schlafen gehen
She is always late for class because she keeps late hours.	
~ **on doing s.th.**	weiterhin etwas tun; fortfahren, etwas zu tun; etwas weiter tun
~ **one's chin up**	den Kopf hinhalten, tapfer handeln/tun
~ **one's hair on** (Brit./Sl.)	ruhig bleiben
~ **one's hand off s.th.**	die Finger von etwas lassen
~ **one's head above water**	sich über Wasser halten (finanziell)
~ **one's nose out of s.th.**	sich aus einer Sache heraushalten
~ **one's temper**	sich beherrschen
~ **one step ahead of s.b.**	jdm. einen Schritt voraus sein
~ **pace with**	Schritt halten mit
~ **quiet**	ruhig bleiben, sich ruhig verhalten
~ **s.o. company**	jdm. Gesellschaft leisten, bei jdm. bleiben
~ **s.o. on tenterhooks**	im Ungewissen lassen, jdn. zappeln lassen
~ **track of s.b.**	jdm. auf der Spur bleiben
~ **up with the Joneses**	mit jdm. Schrritt halten
~ **up with the times**	mit der Zeit gehen, sich auf dem Laufenden halten
~ **your shirt on!** (Sl.)	Hab Geduld! Warte einen Moment!
That's a pretty kettle of fish. (Brit./Sl.)	Das ist eine schöne Bescherung.
kick:	
~ **a habit** (Sl.)	sich etwas abgewöhnen
The drug habit is probably the most difficult to kick.	
~ **one's heels**	warten müssen
~ **over the traces**	über die Stränge schlagen
~ **o.s. (for the doing s.th.)** (Sl.)	sich in den Hintern beißen, etwas bedauern
~ **s.o. out**	jdn. hinauswerfen

~ s.o. upstairs (Sl.)	jdn. befördern
~ the bucket (Sl.)	den Löffel abgeben, abkratzen
~ up (a) dust/a fuss (Sl.)	Staub aufwirbeln
for ~s (Sl.)	zum Spaß
get a ~ out of s.th. (Sl.)	etwas aufregend finden, genießen
~ing and screaming	gegen starken Protest

kid:

~s' stuff (Sl.)	Kinderkram
to ~ s.o.	jdn. veralbern, jdn. ärgern
Don't ~ yourself!	Mach dir nichts vor!
No kidding?	Ehrlich?

kill:

~ the goose that lays the golden eggs	den Ast absägen, auf dem man sitzt
~ the fatted calf	ein Festessen geben, mit viel Aufwand bewirten
~ o.s. doing s.th.	sich mit etwas viel Mühe geben
dressed to ~	aufgetakelt wie eine Fregatte
~ s.o./s.th. off	jdm./etwas ein Ende bereiten
~ s.th. stone dead	eine Sache vollständig zerstören oder beenden
~ time	die Zeit totschlagen
~ two birds with one stone	zwei Fliegen mit einer Klappe schlagen
~ with kindness	jdn. mit Freundlichkeit überhäufen
make a ~ing	viel Geld scheffeln

kind:

~ of	in gewisser Weise, so in etwa
one of a ~	einmalig
two of a ~	zwei, die sich gesucht und gefunden haben

a kindred spirit	eine verwandte Seele

a King Charles's head	ein Thema oder Objekt, auf das sich jmd. dauernd bezieht, unabhängig, ob es mit dem Rest des Gesprächs zu tun hat

king:	
~ of the castle	Anführer
a ~'s ransom	eine sehr große Summe
Kingdom come	Himmel, die nächste Welt
kiss:	
~ the Blarney stone (Brit.)	die Fähigkeit, Leuten schmeicheln und sie überreden zu können
~ of death	der Todesstoß/-kuss
The judge's decision was the kiss of death for our plan.	
~ of life	Mund-zu-Mund-Beatmung
~ the dust (Sl.)	ins Gras beißen
a kitchen-sink drama	ein realistisches Theaterstück über das Leben der Unterklasse
knee-high to a grasshopper	ein kleines Kind
knit one's brows	die Stirn runzeln
knock:	
~ about (Sl.)	herumreisen
He spent his holiday knocking about in Scotland.	
~ against	dagegenschlagen
~ back a drink	ein Getränk runterkippen
~ it off! (Sl.)	Hör auf!
~ out	bewusstlos schlagen
~ s.o.'s block off (Sl.)	jdn. fest auf den Kopf schlagen
~ s.o. into a cocked hat (Sl.)	jdn. locker in die Tasche stecken
~ s.th. (Sl.)	mäkeln, kritisieren
~ the stuffing out of s.o. (Sl.)	jdn. umhauen
a ~ing shop	Bordell
knock-on effect	Kettenreaktion
know:	
~ all the answers	immer alles besser wissen
~ all the tricks of the trade	sich gut auskennen, gerissen sein

~ one's stuff (Sl.)	sich in seinem Fach gut auskennen
She is not the right person for the job, she doesn't know her stuff.	
~ a good thing when one sees one	klug genug sein, den Wert einer Sache beurteilen zu können
~ a hawk from a handsaw	intelligent
~ a thing or two (Brit./Sl.)	schlau sein, weise sein
John is a smart man; he knows a thing or two.	
~ how many beans make five	vernünftig in praktischen Dingen
~ s.th. inside out	etwas in- und auswendig kennen
~ the ropes (Sl.)	wissen, wie etwas läuft/wie eine Sache funktioniert
~ what's what	im Bilde sein
~ which side one's bread is buttered on	wissen, wo seine Interessen liegen
be in the ~	Bescheid wissen
make ~n	bekannt machen
~n all over the place (Sl.)	bekannt wie ein bunter Hund

L

labour:	
~ a point	etwas übermäßig betonen
I understand what you mean, you don't need to labour the point.	
a ~ of love	eine Aufgabe, die man aus Liebe zur Sache übernimmt
~ over s.th.	sich mit etwas abmühen
~ under a delusion	sich täuschen
lag behind	trödeln
Going for a walk with small children is no fun. They quickly lose interest and lag behind.	
laid:	
~ back (Sl.)	gelassen
~ up	1. im Bett (krank), 2. außer Dienst (Reparatur)
1. I've been laid up all week with a bad cold. *2. My car is laid up, it needs a new gearbox.*	
a lame duck	eine Niete
land:	
a ~ flowing with milk and honey	ein Land in dem Milch und Honig fließen; ein Land mit einem Übermaß an natürlichen Ressourcen
the ~ of Nod	im Tiefschlaf
~ on one's feet	auf die Füße fallen
~ s.b. in a mess	jdn. in Schwierigkeiten bringen
~ up as ...	als ... enden
see how the ~ lies	die Lage peilen, sich (diskret) erkundigen
be at large	auf freiem Fuß sein
larger than life	dramatisch übertrieben

last:	
~ but not least	und nicht zuletzt, und nicht zu vergessen
~ night	gestern Abend
the ~ gasp	der letzte Atemzug
the ~ rites	Sterbesakramente
of the ~ importance	von äußerster Wichtigkeit
the ~ but one	der Vorletzte
be on one's ~ legs	auf dem letzten Loch pfeifen
It's the ~ straw that breaks the camel's back. (Sprichw.)	Das ist der Tropfen, der das Fass zum Überlaufen bringt.
at long ~	endlich
the ~ thing at night	vor dem Schlafengehen
the ~ thing one wants	das, was man wirklich nicht will
late:	
~ in life	im fortgeschrittenen Alter
her ~ husband	ihr verstorbener Ehegatte
of ~	in letzter Zeit
better ~ than never	besser zu spät als gar nicht
laugh:	
~ up one's sleeve (Sl.)	sich ins Fäustchen lachen
have the last ~	das letzte Wort haben
~ at s.b.	jdn. auslachen
~ s.th. off	mit einem Lachen über etwas hinweggehen
~ like a drain	sich ausschütten vor Lachen
~, and the world ~s with you weep, and you weep alone. (Sprichw.)	Lache und die Welt ist dein, weine und du bist allein.
You'll ~ on the other side of your face.	Dir wird das Lachen schon vergehen.
He ~s best who ~s last. (Sprichw.)	Wer zuletzt lacht, lacht am besten.
just for ~s	nur zum Spaß
the laughing academy	Irrenanstalt
rest on one's laurels	sich auf seinen Lorbeeren ausruhen

lay:	
~ by for a rainy day	einen Notgroschen beiseite legen
~ aside one's worries	seine Sorgen hinter sich lassen
~ claim to s.th.	auf etwas Anspruch erheben
~ a trap for s.b.	jdm. eine Falle stellen
The police laid a trap for the criminal and he walked into it.	
~ hold of s.th.	etwas in die Hand nehmen, anpacken
I can't wait to lay hold of that spade and help you dig the garden.	
~ it on thick	übertreiben
I don't believe half of what you say. You always lay it on thick.	
~ in food supplies	Hamsterkäufe tätigen, Essensvorräte anlegen
~ off s.o. (Sl.)	jdn. in Ruhe lassen
~ s.o. off	jdn. entlassen
~ plans	Pläne machen
~ on a party	eine Party veranstalten
~ one's cards on the table	die Karten auf den Tisch legen
~ one's hands on s.th.	etwas in die Hände bekommen, erwischen
I'll really tell him off when I lay hands on him.	
~ s.th. on thick	etwas dick auftragen
~ s.th. at s.b.'s door	jdm. die Schuld für etwas anlasten
~ s.th. bare	eine Sache aufdecken
~ stress on s.th.	etwas betonen
~ the blame for s.th. on s.b.	jdm. die Schuld für eine Sache in die Schuhe schieben
lead:	
~ a dog's life	ein Hundeleben führen
~ astray	auf den falschen Weg führen, fehlleiten
~ a busy life	beschäftigt sein, viel zu tun haben
~ s.b. a dance	jdn. an der Nase herumführen
~ off	die Führung übernehmen, den Anfang machen

~ on	ermutigen, aufmuntern
~ up the garden path	jdn. an der Nase herumführen
~ up to	anleiten, überleiten zu, nach sich ziehen
~ the life of Riley (Sl.)	in Luxus leben
~ two lives	ein Doppelleben führen
~ the way	jdm. den richtigen Weg zeigen
a ~ing light	eine herausragende Persönlichkeit
leaf:	
shake like ~	wie Espenlaub zittern
~ through	durchblättern
take a ~ out of s.o.'s book	jdm. etwas nachmachen, wie jdn. handeln
turn over a new ~	ein neues Leben anfangen
lean over backwards to do s.th.	sich die größte Mühe geben, etwas zu tun; sich fast umbringen, etwas zu tun
leap:	
~ at the chance	die Gelegenheit beim Schopf ergreifen
by ~s and bounds	sprunghaft
learn:	
~ a lesson	etwas aus Erfahrung lernen
~ by heart	auswendig lernen
~ by rote	auswendig lernen
~ s.th. the hard way	aus (bitterer) Erfahrung lernen
enjoy a new lease of life	neu aufleben
least:	
the ~ one can do	das Mindeste, was man tun kann
~ said, soonest mended. (Sprichw.)	Reden ist Silber, Schweigen ist Gold.
be tough as old leather	zäh wie Leder sein

leave:

~ alone	in Ruhe lassen
~ a lot to be desired	sehr viel zu wünschen übrig lassen
~ no stone unturned	nichts unversucht lassen
~ off	aufhören, ablassen
~ s.b. to himself/to his own devices	jdn. sich selbst überlassen
~ s.o. in the lurch	jdn. im Stich lassen
~ s.o. out in the cold	jdn. ausschließen
~ s.th. to chance	etwas dem Zufall überlassen
~ it at that	es dabei belassen
~ it out! (Sl.)	Kommt nicht in Frage!
~ word with s.o.	eine Nachricht hinterlassen
take one's ~	seinen Abschied nehmen
take ~ of one's senses	von allen guten Geistern verlassen sein

Hove you taken leave of your senses, driving my car into the ditch!

left:

~ and right	in alle Richtungen
~, right and centre	überall
a ~-handed remark/compliment	ein zweifelhaftes, fragwürdiges Kompliment

leg:

not to have a ~ to stand on	etwas nicht entschuldigen können
to be on one's last ~	am Ende sein

lend:

~ one's ear	ein Ohr leihen, zuhören
~ s.b. a hand	jdm. zur Hand gehen
~ o.s. to s.th.	sich zu etwas hergeben, bei etwas mitmachen

This kind of plan is not one I could lend myself to.

length:

the ~ and breadth of s.th.	das ganze Gebiet
at great ~	lang und breit, ausführlich

The professor always spoke at great length about nothing at all.

at ~	nach einiger Zeit, mit der Zeit
At length, he got up and left the room.	
For what ~ of time?	Für wie lange?
go to any ~s	über Leichen gehen
He will go to any lengths to get what he wants.	
the lesser of two evils	das Geringere von zwei Übeln
let:	
~ alone	1. nicht berühren, sich nicht einmischen, 2. geschweige denn
1. Let it well alone. That's none of our business.	
2. I didn't ask Mary, let alone the rest of the family.	
~ a person off s.th.	jdm. etwas erlassen, jdn. entbinden von
Let bygones be bygones. (Sprichw.)	Schwamm drüber; lass die Vergangenheit ruhen
~ grass grow under one's feet	still stehen, nichts tun
John is always busy, he doesn't let the grass grow under his feet.	
~ off steam	Dampf ablassen, explodieren
~ down	1. enttäuschen, im Stich lassen, 2. die Luft aus den Reifen lassen
1. He promised never to let her down.	
2. He let the tyre of her bicycle down.	
~ go!	Lass los!
~ it go at that	es dabei bewenden lassen
~ o.s. in for s.th.	sich auf etwas einlassen
Let sleeping dogs lie. (Sprichw.)	Schlafende Hunde soll man nicht wecken.
~ s.o. off the hook	jdn. verschonen
~ s.th. slide (Sl.)	etwas vernachlässigen
~ s.th. slip	eine Bemerkung fallen lassen, etwas verraten
~ the cat out of the bag	ein Geheimnis lüften, die Katze aus dem Sack lassen

I wasn't supposed to know about the party but my sister let the cat out of the bag.

the letter of the law	der Wortlaut des Gesetzes

level:

do one's ~ best	sein Möglichstes tun
have/keep a ~ head	einen kühlen Kopf haben/ behalten
on the ~	ehrlich
~ with s.o. (Sl.)	zu jdm. ehrlich sein

lick:

~ s.b.'s boot	jdm. die Stiefel küssen
~ one's lips	sich die Lippen lecken
a ~ of paint	eine Schicht Farbe
~ one's wounds	sich die Wunden lecken
~ s.th. into shape (Sl.)	etwas formen, salonfähig (vorzeigbar) machen

The garden looks a terrible mess, but we'll soon lick it into shape.

lie:

~ awake	wach liegen
~ doggo (Sl.)	sich verstecken
~ down on the job	nicht aufpassen, etwas schlecht erledigen

I have to keep an eye on the workmen, I don't want them lying down on the job.

~ low (Sl.)	sich ruhig und unauffällig verhalten
tell a ~	lügen
~ through one's teeth	dreist lügen (überzeugend)
give the ~ to	absolut widersprechen

His behaviour gave the lie to what he said.

~ at s.o.'s door	für etwas verantwortlich sein
~ in store for	auf jdn. warten
a white ~	eine harmlose Lüge

life:

~ begins at forty. (Sprichw.)	Mit vierzig fängt das Leben an.
~ is not a bed of roses	das Leben ist nicht einfach
~ is worth living	man genießt das Leben
Sitting there on the beach with a drink in his hand, life certainly was worth living.	
for ~	lebenslänglich
have the time of one's ~	etwas sehr genießen, eine wunderbare Zeit haben
not for the ~ of me	nicht um alles in der Welt
not on your ~!	nie und nimmer! auf gar keinen Fall!
seek s.o.'s ~	jdm. nach dem Leben trachten
be the ~ and soul of the party	der Mittelpunkt des Festes sein
in the prime of ~	im besten Alter
as large as ~	in voller Größe

lift:

give s.b. a ~	jdn. (per Anhalter) mitnehmen
~ a hand against s.o.	jdm. Schläge androhen
not ~ a finger	keinen Finger rühren
He never even lifted a finger to help me.	

light:

the ~ of day	bei Tageslicht
cast some ~ on s.th.	erklären, Licht in eine Sache bringen
come to ~	ans Tageslicht kommen, aufgedeckt werden
His treachery only came to light after his death.	
in a good ~	günstig, in günstigem Licht
in the ~ of	in Anbetracht ...
~ upon	durch Zufall entdecken
make ~ a work of s.th.	ein anderes Licht auf etwas werfen
make ~ of	bagatellisieren
He always makes light of his disability.	
to see the ~	die Wahrheit erkennen, Erleuchtung erlangen (oft iron.)

lighten up (Sl.)	entspannen, etwas nicht so schwer nehmen
like:	
and one's ~	seinesgleichen
and the ~	und Ähnliches
The farmer gave us fresh bread, butter, apples, pears and the like.	
~ anything!	(bekräftigend:) Aber wie!
~ a bat out of hell	wie ein geölter Blitz
~ billy-o (Sl.)	energisch, erfolgreich
~ blazes	so stark wie möglich
~ a bolt out of the blue (Sl.)	wie ein Blitz aus heiterem Himmel
~ a bull at the gate	aggressiv, direkt
~ a bull in a china shop	wie ein Elefant im Porzellanladen
~ calls to ~	Gleich und gleich gesellt sich gern.
~ a cat on hot bricks	wie die Katze auf dem heißen Blechdach
~ the cat that stole the cream	selbstzufrieden
~ Caesar's wife	keusch, anständig
~ the clappers	geräuschvoll
~ the curate's egg	eine Sache hat gute und schlechte Teile
~ a dog with two tails	begeistert, zufrieden mit sich selbst
~ father, ~ son. (Sprichw.)	Wie der Vater, so der Sohn.
~ a fish out of water	fehl am Platz, ungeschickt
~ a fishwife	laut, vulgär
~ a fly in amber	unverändert erhalten
~ greased lightning	wie ein geölter Blitz
~ hell it is	so ist es absolut nicht
It is all right!	
Like hell it is!	
~ it or lump it (Sl.)	Vogel friss oder stirb, eine Sache entweder akzeptieren/einsehen oder einfach hinnehmen
~ a hot knife through butter	ohne jeden Widerstand
~ a lamb	ohne Protest, brav
~ nobody's business	mit größter Intensität
as ~ as two peas in a pod	wie ein Ei dem anderen gleichen

~ a sack of potatoes	wie ein Sack Kartoffeln
~ a stuck pig	wie ein angestochenes Schwein
~ a ton of bricks	mit großer Wucht oder Ernsthaftigkeit
~ water off a duck's back	ohne sichtbaren Erfolg, ohne Eindruck zu machen
~ wildfire	weitreichend und mit großer Geschwindigkeit
That's just ~ him.	Das sieht ihm ähnlich.
That's more ~ it.	Das ist doch schon besser!
There is nothing ~ ...	Es geht nichts über ...
What is she ~?	Wie ist sie?
a likely story	(iron.) eine unwahrscheinliche Geschichte
likes:	
~ and dislikes	Vorlieben und Abneigungen
the ~ of s.b.	Leute wie ...
The likes of the Harveys do not go to church unless they can be sure of an audience, you know.	
That's about the limit. (Sl.)	Das ist der absolute Hammer.
line:	
~ one's own pockets	auf unredliche Weise Geld verdienen
be in ~ with	übereinstimmen mit
fall into ~ with s.b.	sich jdm. anschließen
~ up	sich anstellen
put s.th. on the ~	Klartext über eine Sache reden
stand in ~	in einer Reihe stehen
take the ~ of least resistance	den Weg des geringsten Widerstandes gehen
way out of ~	absolut nicht in Ordnung
lion:	
the ~ lies down with the lamb	Frieden und Ruhe herrschen
the ~'s share	der Löwenanteil
live:	
~ it up	sich ein schönes Leben machen

~ like a lord (Sl.)	auf großem Fuß leben
~ above/beyond one's means	über seine Verhältnisse leben
~ and let live	leben und leben lassen
~ on	sich ernähren von
~ through s.th.	etwas durchmachen
~ to see the day	etwas noch erleben
You have to ~ with it.	Du musst dich damit abfinden/ damit leben.
~ up to s.th.	Erwartungen erfüllen, sich als würdig erweisen
You have just given me such a good reference, I hope I can live up to it.	
lo and behold!	Sieh da!
a load of rubbish	Unfug
lock:	
~ the stable door after the horse has bolted	Wer zu spät kommt, den bestraft das Leben.
~, stock and barrel	alles, mit allem Drum und Dran
I finished the job at last, lock, stock and barrel.	
Lombard street to a China orange	die Wahrscheinlichkeit ist deutlich in einer bestimmten Richtung
a lone wolf	ein einsamer Wolf; jmd., der so weit wie möglich ohne andere Menschen lebt oder arbeitet
Lonely Hearts	einsame Herzen
long^1:	
the ~ arm of the law	die weitreichende Autorität des Gesetzes
in the ~ run	letztendlich
~ ago	vor langer Zeit
~ time no see. (Sl.)	Lange nicht gesehen!
a ~ shot	nur eine Vermutung, nicht sehr wahrscheinlich

by a ~ shot	bei Weitem
the ~ and the short of it	kurz und gut
The long and the short of it is that you just can't hope to win.	
~-standing	lang geplant/ausgemacht
I have a long-standing invitation to a concert this evening.	
~-suffering	geduldig, ausdauernd
~-winded	langatmig
so ~ (Sl.)	bis dann, später

long²:

~ for s.th.	sich nach etwas sehnen

look:

~ as if butter would not melt in s.b.'s mouth	sehr korrekt wirken
~ as if one has been dragged through a hedge backwards	unordentlich, verwüstet
have a good ~ at s.th.	sich etwas genau ansehen
~ s.o. in the eye	jdm. ins Gesicht sehen
I don't like the ~ of it.	Die Sache gefällt mir ganz und gar nicht.
it ~s like	es sieht so aus, als ob
~ after s.b.	sich um jdn. kümmern
~ ahead	in die Zukunft blicken
~ daggers at s.o. (Sl.)	jdn. böse anschauen
~ down on s.b.	auf jdn. herabsehen
~ for	suchen nach
~ forward	sich freuen auf
~ for trouble (Sl.)	Schwierigkeiten heraufbeschwören
The policeman told me to leave, unless I was looking for trouble.	
~ here!	Na hören Sie mal!
~ into s.th.	einer Sache nachgehen
The headmaster promised to look into the matter.	
~ in on s.o.	bei jdm. vorbeischauen
~ s.th. up	etwas nachschlagen
~ on s.b. as	jdn. betrachten als, jdn. halten für
I look on him as a friend.	

~ down one's nose at s.o.	auf jdn. herabsehen
~ out!	Vorsicht! Pass auf!
~ out for s.b.	nach jdm. Ausschau halten
Look out for John when you're in London.	
~ over s.th.	etwas durchsehen
~ the other way	angestrengt wegsehen
~ up to s.o.	zu jdm. aufblicken

loose:

~ ends	offene Probleme
~ talk	Klatsch und Tratsch
at a ~ end	faul, untätig, ohne bestimmtes Ziel
have a ~ tongue	eine lose Zunge haben
have a slate ~	eine Schraube locker haben

lord:

~ it over s.o.	sich arrogant benehmen, wichtig tun
The head of department lords it over his assistants.	
~ and master	Herrscher, Befehlshaber
the ~s of creation	1. die Menschheit, 2. Männer (im Gegensatz zu Frauen)

lose:

~ face	das Gesicht verlieren, sich blamieren
~ it (Sl.)	wirr/wütend werden
~ one's cool (Am./Sl.)	böse/wütend werden
~ heart	den Mut verlieren
~ it's looks	schlechter aussehen als vorher
~ one's marbles (Sl.)	verrückt werden
~ one's mind	verrückt werden
~ one's rag	unbeherrscht reagieren, seinen Ärger offen zeigen
~ one's shirt (Sl.)	sein letztes Hemd verlieren
~ one's temper	wütend werden
~ one's train of thought	den Faden verlieren
~ one's tongue	sprachlos sein, es verschlägt einem die Sprache
~ sight of	aus den Augen verlieren

~ touch with	nicht mehr auf dem Laufenden sein, den Kontakt verlieren
be at a loss	in Verlegenheit sein
lost:	
a ~ cause	eine verlorene Sache
a ~ soul	die Seele eines Sünders
~ in thought	in Gedanken verloren/vertieft
a lot of water has run under the bridge	viel Wasser ist den Bach herunter geflossen
loud:	
~ and long	laut und anhaltend
~ and clear	klar und deutlich
love:	
~ is blind. (Sprichw.)	Liebe macht blind.
~ me, ~ my dog	Wer micht liebt, liebt auch meinen Hund.
fall in ~	sich verlieben
Give my ~ to ...!	Grüße bitte ... von mir.
~ doing s.th.	etwas sehr gerne tun
play for ~	nicht um Geld spielen
~ at first sight	Liebe auf den ersten Blick
The ~ of money is the root of all evil. (Sprichw.)	Geldgier ist die Wurzel allen Übels.
not for ~ or money	nicht für Geld und gute Worte, keineswegs, überhaupt nicht
I've tried all the libraries, but I can't find the book for love or money.	
no ~ lost between	sich nicht grün sein/mögen
a low profile	unauffällig
lower one's sights	seine Ansprüche senken
luck:	
bad ~!	So ein Pech!
It's the ~ of the draw.	Man muss es so nehmen, wie's kommt.

Just my ~!	Pech gehabt, wie immer!
lucky:	
~ at cards, unlucky in love. (Sprichw.)	Glück im Spiel, Pech in der Liebe.
a ~ dip	Glückstopf
lumber s.o. with s.th. (Sl.)	jdn. mit etwas belasten
If you don't like it, you can lump it!	Damit wirst du dich abfinden müssen.
out to lunch (Sl.)	verrückt

M

mad:	
~ about s.th.	verrückt nach etwas sein
~ as a hatter	vollkommen übergeschnappt
like ~ (Sl.)	wie verrückt
He's been playing tennis like mad all morning.	
drive s.o. ~	jdn. verrückt machen
be ~ on/about s.o./s.th.	verrückt nach jdm. sein, etwas sehr gerne tun
go ~	wahnsinnig werden

make:	
~ answer	antworten
~ an appearance	auftauchen, präsent sein
~ a beginning	einen Anfang machen
~ a beeline for	auf jdn./etwas geradewegs zugehen
He entered the room and made a beeline for his wife.	
~ bold to do s.th.	etwas wagen
~ both ends meets	sich nach der Decke strecken
You can't ~ bricks without straw. (Sprichw.)	Mit nichts kann man kein Haus bauen.
~ a cat laugh	außergewöhnlich komisch sein
~ certain	sicherstellen
~ a change	1. etwas ändern 2. eine Abwechslung bieten
1. He made changes in the department as soon as he was appointed. *2. The new theatre certainly made a change in the cultural environment.*	
~ s.th. clear	deutlich machen
~ a deal with	ein Abkommen treffen mit
~ an example of s.b.	an jdm. ein Exempel statuieren
~ a face	Grimassen schneiden
~ fast	befestigen, anbinden
~ one's fortune	reich werden

~ a fuss about s.th.	viel Aufhebens um etwas machen
~ a go of s.th. (Sl.)	etwas erfolgreich tun
~ a good job of s.th.	gute Arbeit leisten
~ a good showing	sich ordentlich benehmen, den Erwartungen entsprechen
~ great strides	sich deutlich verbessern
~ a habit of s.th.	sich etwas zur Gewohnheit machen
~ a mountain out of a molehill. (Sprichw.)	Aus einer Mücke einen Elefanten machen.
~ a name for o.s.	sich einen Namen machen, bekannt werden
~ a song and dance of s.th.	ein fürchterliches Theater wegen etwas machen
~ do with s.th.	sich mit etwas behelfen
~ eyes at s.o.	jdm. schöne Augen machen
~ friends with	sich anfreunden
~ good money	gut verdienen
~ good use of s.th.	etwas richtig anwenden/ einsetzen
~ haste!	Beeil dich!
~ it	einen Termin schaffen
~ light of s.th.	etwas verniedlichen, herunterspielen
~ one's way in the world	seinen Weg machen
~ peace	Frieden schließen
~ shift with	sich behelfen mit
~ s.th. a rule	sich etwas zur Regel machen
~ s.th. up	etwas erfinden, sich etwas ausdenken
~ s.th.	es schaffen, zu etwas zu kommen (zu einer Einladung, Verabredung etc.)
We were sorry you couldn't come to the party but hope you'll make it next time.	
~ the best of a bad job	gute Miene zum bösen Spiel machen
~ the grade	es schaffen, Erwartungen entsprechen
It is very important to make the grade if you want to be successful in business.	

~ the most of one's life	das Beste aus seinem Leben machen, sein Leben in vollen Zügen genießen
~ tracks for home	sich auf den Heimweg machen
~ up for lost time	verlorene Zeit wieder wettmachen
~ up one's mind	sich entschließen, eine Entscheidung treffen
~ way for	vorbeigehen lassen, Platz machen
~ one's way	vorankommen

man:

~ and beast	Mensch und Tier
~ and boy	sein ganzes Leben lang, von Kindheit an
I have been living in this part of town, man and boy, for thirty-nine years now.	
the ~ for the job	für eine Aufgabe geeignet
the ~ in the street	der Mann von der Straße
a ~ of few words	schweigsam
a ~ of God	Geistlicher
the ~ of the house	Hausherr
a ~ of letters	Dichter, Schriftsteller
a ~ of many parts	vielseitig begabt
a ~ of substance	wohlhabend
a ~ of the world	ein Mann von Welt
Man proposes but God disposes. (Sprichw.)	Der Mensch denkt, Gott lenkt.
~'s inhumanity to ~	die Bereitschaft der Menschen, einander Böses zu tun

many:

~ a one	manch einer
~ a long day	eine lange Zeit, eine Ewigkeit
We have not seen them for many a long day.	
~ are called but few are chosen	Viele sind berufen, aber wenige sind auserwählt.
~ hands make light work.	Viele Hände, wenig Arbeit.
~ happy returns of the day	herzlichen Glückwunsch zum Geburtstag
~ a little makes a mickle. (Sprichw.)	Kleinvieh macht auch Mist.

~ a time	regelmäßig, oft
off the map (Sl.)	hinter dem Mond, abgelegen
a mare's nest	ein Reinfall
Tell that to the Marines. (Sl.)	Das mach' einem anderen weis.
mark:	
overstep the ~	zu weit gehen
up to the ~	gesundheitlich in Ordnung
~ time	auf der Stelle bleiben, nicht voran kommen
~ my words	erinnert euch daran, was ich sage
a marked person	auf der schwarzen Liste stehen
marriage:	
a ~ of convenience	eine Hochzeit aus Vernunftsgründen
a ~ of true minds	eine geistige Ehe
marry:	
~ in haste, repent at leisure. (Sprichw.)	Heiraten in Eile bereut man mit Weile.
~ money	reich heiraten
matter:	
a ~ of s.th.	es ist eine Frage von
a ~ of concern	Anlass zur Sorge
as a ~ of course	entsprechend der üblichen Abläufe
What's the ~?	Was ist los?
as a ~ of fact	in der Tat
a ~ of the moment	ein Problem von erheblicher Wichtigkeit
a ~ of opinion	Ansichtssache
a ~ of time	eine Frage der Zeit
no ~ what	egal was
it doesn't ~	das macht nichts
~-of-fact	hart, geschäftsmäßig, ohne Gefühle

He broke the sad news in a very matter-of-fact voice.	
not mince ~s	kein Blatt vor den Mund nehmen
mean:	
~ business	es ernst meinen
by all ~s	aber bitte sehr (als wohlwollende Zusage), unter allen Umständen
by no ~s	auf keinen Fall
~ well	es gut meinen
~ to do s.th.	vorhaben, etwas zu tun
I have been meaning to phone you all week.	
the means to an end	die nötigen Mittel, um ein bestimmtes Ergebnis zu erzielen
meanwhile, back at the ranch	um zu der eigentlichen Geschichte zurückzukehren
measure one's length	der Länge nach hinfallen
meet:	
~ one's end	sterben
~ with	bekommen, erhalten
He met with great sympathy when his wife died.	
~ one's maker	sterben
~ one's match	seinen Meister finden
make ends ~	sich nach der Decke strecken
No matter how much I save, I don't seem to be able to make ends meet.	
more than ~s the eye	mehr, als man auf Anhieb erkennen kann
~ s.b. halfway	jdm. auf halbem Weg entgegenkommen
~ s.b.'s eye	den Blick erwidern
~ with an accident	verunglücken
s.b.'s memory is green	jmd. ist nach seinem Tode nicht vergessen

mend:	
~ one's ways	sich bessern (im moralischen Sinne)
~ one's manners	seine Manieren verbessern
Don't mention it!	Schon gut, nicht der Rede wert!
mess:	
be in a ~ (Sl.)	in der Tinte sitzen
~ about with s.th.	an etwas herumbasteln
~ s.th. up (Sl.)	Mist machen
~ s.o. about (Sl.)	jdm. die Zeit stehlen
~ s.o. up (Sl.)	jdn. verprügeln
take the micky (Sl.)	jdn. veralbern
might:	
~ as well	auch gleich
If you are going shopping, you might as well take the dog.	
~ is right.	Wer die Macht hat, der hat auch das Recht.
a mile off	weit weg
milk:	
~ s.o. dry	jdn. nach Strich und Faden ausnehmen
the ~ of human kindness	Güte
~-and-water	seicht, verwässert
a millstone round s.o.'s neck (Sl.)	ein Klotz am Bein
run of the mill (Sl.)	08/15, alltäglich
mind:	
a ~ to	Wunsch, Bedürfnis
I've a good mind to complain to the company.	
be in two ~s about s.th.	sich über etwas im Unklaren sein
Do you ~!	Muss das denn sein!
give s.o. a piece of one's ~ (Brit.)	jdm. gehörig die Meinung sagen
have s.th. in ~	etwas vorhaben, einen Plan haben

know one's ~	wissen, was man will
make up one's ~	sich entschließen
Never ~!	Das macht nichts!
read s.b.'s ~	jds. Gedanken lesen
speak one's ~	sagen, was man denkt
~ one's own business	sich um die eigenen Angelegenheiten kümmern
have a one-track ~ *The only thing Eric thinks about is money, he has such a one-track mind.*	immer nur das eine im Sinn haben
~ one's P's and Q's	sich anständig benehmen
out of one's ~	wahnsinnig, von Sinnen
~ you	aber andererseits (im Sinne einer Einschränkung)
a mine of information	eine Quelle des Wissens
miss:	
A ~ is as good as a mile. (Sprichw.)	Knapp daneben ist auch vorbei.
~ the boat (Sl.)	der Zug ist abgefahren, den Anschluss verpassen
~ the mark	daneben liegen, falsch liegen
~ the train	den Zug verpassen
~ one's footing	ausrutschen, stolpern
~ the point	nicht verstehen, worum es geht
give s.th. a ~	die Finger von etwas lassen
It's a mixed blessing.	Das ist ein zweischneidiges Schwert
just a mo' (Sl.)	sofort, gleich
moan and groan	sich beschweren
moment:	
the ~ of truth	die Stunde der Wahrheit
in a ~	bald, gleich
unguarded ~ *In an unguarded moment, he gave his secret away.*	ein unachtsamer Augenblick

money:

~ is no object.	Geld spielt keine Rolle.
for my ~	meiner Ansicht nach
pocket-~	Taschengeld
put one's money where one's mouth is	seinen Worten Taten folgen lassen

monkey:

~ business	Unfug
not to give a ~'s about s.th. (Sl.)	sich einen Dreck um etwas scheren

a moonlight flit	bei Nacht und Nebel ausziehen

Why are you packing your suitcases? Are you thinking of a moonfight flit?

a moot point	ein strittiger Punkt

more:

the ~ the merrier	je mehr desto besser
~ royalist than the king	katholischer als der Papst
~ sinned against than sinning	jmd. hat mehr Unrecht erlitten als begangen
~ or less	mehr oder weniger
to be ~ to s.th. than ...	an etwas ist mehr dran, als ...

morning:

the ~-after feeling	die Katerstimmung am nächsten Morgen
~, noon and night	immer wieder; morgens, mittags, abends

the most one can say	das Beste, was man sagen kann

mother:

be tied to one's ~'s apron-strings	der Mutter am Rockzipfel hängen
a ~'s boy	ein Muttersöhnchen

mountain:

The ~ labours and brings forth a mouse.	Viel Mühe, wenig Nutzen.

If the ~ will not come to Mohammed, then Mohammed must go to the ~. (Sprichw.)	Wenn der Prophet nicht zum Berg kommt, kommt der Berg zum Propheten.
mouth:	
one's ~ waters	jdm. läuft das Wasser im Munde zusammen
down in the ~	niedergeschlagen
move:	
Get a ~ on!	Spute dich!
~ heaven and earth	Himmel und Hölle in Bewegung setzen
~ house	umziehen
~ up in the world	erfolgreich sein, avancieren
Mr Right	Märchenprinz
Mrs Grundy	eine engstirnige und humorlose Person
Mrs Mop	Putzfrau
much:	
~ good as it may do	möge es ihm nützen
~ mistaken	im Irrtum
~ of a muchness	sehr ähnlich
I'm not ~ of a ...	Ich bin kein großer ...
Mud sticks. (Sprichw.)	Etwas bleibt immer hängen.
That's a mug's game!	Das ist doch schwachsinnig!
mum:	
~'s the word!	Kein Wort darüber!
to keep ~	den Mund halten

N

nail:	
be a ~ in s.b.'s coffin	ein Nagel zu jds. Sarg sein, das Ende oder Scheitern von jdm. beschleunigen
~ s.o. down	jdn. festnageln
I tried to nail him down as to the time of his arrival.	
as hard as ~s	knallhart
hit the ~ on the head	den Nagel auf den Kopf treffen
on the ~ (Sl.)	pünktlich, sofort
have a narrow escape	gerade noch davonkommen
one's native heath	Heimatort
near:	
be ~ at hand	in der Nähe/in Reichweite/ zur Hand sein
a ~ thing	gerade noch mal Glück haben, ein knappes Entkommen
That was a near thing. You almost dropped that antique vase.	
draw ~	es geht auf ... zu
Christmas draws near, we must buy a tree and decorate it.	
~ the mark	beinahe richtig
That wasn't quite the right answer but it was very near the mark.	
be ~ and dear	jdm. nahe stehen
one's ~est and dearest	Familie
the ~est offer	der höchste gebotene Preis
a necessary evil	ein notwendiges Übel
Necessity is the mother of invention. (Sprichw.)	Not macht erfinderisch.
neck:	
~ and ~	Kopf an Kopf

get it in the ~ (Brit./Sl.)	bestraft werden
~ and crop	vollständig
~ or nothing	Kopf und Kragen für den Erfolg riskieren
need:	
~ one's head examined	nicht ganz bei Trost, dumm
~ s.th. like one ~s a hole in the head	etwas brauchen wie einen Kropf
~ a long spoon to eat with the devil.	Wer mit dem Teufel essen will, muss einen langen Löffel haben.
~ no introduction	als bekannt voraussetzen können
a needle in a haystack	die Nadel im Heuhaufen
neither:	
~ here nor there	das spielt keine Rolle
~ hide nor hair of s.b.	keine Spur von jdm.
nerve:	
You have got a ~! (Sl.)	Du hast vielleicht Nerven!
have the ~ to do s.th.	die Frechheit besitzen, etwas zu tun
a nervous wreck	mit den Nerven am Ende
the net result	das Endergebnis
never:	
~ fear	nur keine Bange
~ mind!	Lass gut sein, vergiss es!
well, I ~!	kaum zu glauben!
new:	
~ blood	Anfänger, neue Leute
A ~ broom (sweeps clean).	(Sprichw.) Neue Besen kehren besser.
a ~ deal	ein gesellschaftliches oder politisches Reformprogramm
news:	
be ~ to s.o.	jdm. noch nicht bekannt sein
be bad ~	Ärger bringen

~ from nowhere	nichts Neues, bereits bekannt
the good ~ is	die gute Nachricht ist

next:

the ~ best thing to s.th.	fast so gut wie
the ~ but one	der Übernächste
~ to nothing	fast nichts, sehr wenig

nice:

~ one, Cyril	Nicht schlecht gemacht!
~ weather for ducks	Regenwetter
~ work if you can get it	Ausdruck von Neid auf etwas, das jmd. anderes erhalten hat

nick:

in the ~ of time	gerade noch rechtzeitig
to ~ s.o. (Sl.)	jdn. verhaften
to ~ s.th. (Sl.)	etwas stehlen

night:

make a ~ of it	die Nacht durchmachen
a ~ out	ein Abend unterwegs

nine:

~ times out of ten	fast immer
a ~ to five job	eine geregelte Tätigkeit

nip:

It was ~ and tuck.	Das war eine knappe Sache.
~ in	bei jdm. vorbeischauen
~ s.th. in the bud	im Keim ersticken

get down to the nitty-gritty	zur Sache kommen

no:

~ doubt	sicher, ohne Zweifel
~ laughing matter	eine ernste Sache
To lose one's wallet on the underground is no laughing matter.	
~ skin off s.o.'s back	kein Problem sein

none:

~ the less	trotzdem

~ other than	kein anderer als
~ so blind as those who will not see. (Sprichw.)	Keiner ist blinder als der nicht sehen will.
~ too	nicht sehr
The dog was none too bright, but it would serve to play with the kids.	
~ too soon	im letzten Moment
nooks and crannies	kleine Ecken und Winkel
nose:	
~ about	schnüffeln
follow one's ~	immer der Nase nach
~ s.th. out	etwas aufstöbern/aufdecken
turn one's ~ up at s.th.	die Nase über etwas rümpfen
My cat turns up its nose at tinned food, it only eats fresh meat.	
under s.o.'s ~	vor der Nase von jdm.
~ for s.th.	nach etwas schnüffeln
~ around	herumschnüffeln, Nachforschungen anstellen
not:	
~ see wood for trees	vor lauter Bäumen den Wald nicht sehen
~ born yesterday	nicht von gestern
~ hold water (Sl.)	keinen Sinn ergeben
Your argument doesn't convince me, it doesn't hold water.	
~ sleep a wink	kein Auge zutun
strike the note	den richtigen Ton anschlagen
nothing:	
~ in particular	nichts Besonderes
~ doing! (Sl.)	Nichts da! Kommt nicht in Frage!
~ of the kind	absolut nichts, nichts dergleichen
~ short of	absolut
~ to it	einfach, leicht
~ to write home about (Sl.)	nichts Aufregendes/Besonderes
I can make ~ of it.	Damit kann ich nichts anfangen.

now:	
~ and again	hin und wieder, von Zeit zu Zeit
~ or never	jetzt oder nie
~ it can be told	inzwischen kann man es offen sagen
~ you're talking!	Stimmt! Gute Idee!
nowhere:	
~ to be seen	nirgends zu sehen
~ special	irgendwo
the nub of the matter	der springende Punkt
make o.s. a nuisance	lästig werden, zu einer Plage werden
null and void	wirkungslos, nicht bindend
number one *Jack was busy looking after number one, so of course he could not help us!*	die eigene Person
nurse a grievance	lange über einem ärgerlichen Anlass brüten
nut:	
go off one's ~	verrückt werden
a hard ~ to crack *The detective was having difficulty with a case. It was a hard nut to crack.*	eine harte Nuss
nuts:	
drive s.b. ~	jdn. verrückt machen
~ about s.o.	nach jdm. verrückt sein
in a nutshell	kurz zusammengefasst
nutty as a fruitcake (Sl.)	total verrückt

O

object:	
an ~ lesson	praktische Unterweisung
the ~ of one's affection	Geliebte(r)
be obliged to s.o.	jdm. sehr verbunden sein
occur to s.o.	jdm. einfallen
odd:	
~s and ends	Kleinkram
an ~ bird	eine exzentrische Person
~ jobs	verschiedene Aufgaben
~s and sods	wertloses Zeug
against all ~s	entgegen aller Erwartungen
be at ~s with s.b.	mit jdm. auf Kriegsfuß stehen
s.th. makes no ~s	etwas spielt keine Rolle
the ~ man out	Außenseiter, das fünfte Rad am Wagen
The ~s are against you.	Die Chancen stehen schlecht für dich. Du bist im Nachteil.
What's the ~s? (Sl.)	Was macht das schon?
of:	
~ all the nerve!	So eine Frechheit!
~ academic interest	ohne praktischen Wert, bedeutungslos
~ course (not)	selbstverständlich (nicht)
~ the first magnitude	von äußerster Wichtigkeit
If that should happen, it would truly be a catastrophe of the first magnitude.	
~ good standing	mit einem guten Ruf
~ late	in letzter Zeit
~ no avail	ohne Ergebnis
~ necessity	notwendigerweise, gezwungenermaßen
~ note	bekannt
~ the old school	vom alten Schlag
~ the order ~	etwa

A saving in fuel of the order of at least ten per cent is expected.

~ one's own accord	spontan, freiwillig
~ the same stripe	zur gleichen Gruppe gehörig

off:

~ and on	gelegentlich
~-day (Sl.)	Pechtag
~ duty	dienstfrei
~-hand	leichthin, lässig
~ limits	Zutritt verboten
~-putting	unsympathisch, unkooperativ
~ the map	am Ende der Welt
~ the record	im Vertrauen
~ the beaten track	abseits, abgelegen
~ the cuff	spontan, ohne Übung
~ to (Sl.)	unterwegs nach
be ~ sick	sich krankgemeldet haben
on the ~-chance	in der leisen Hoffnung
tell s.o. ~	jdn. zusammenstauchen

oil:

~ s.b.'s palm	jdm. Schmiergelder zukommen lassen, jdn. bestechen
pour ~ on the flames	Öl ins Feuer gießen
~ and water do not mix. (Sprichw.)	Wasser und Feuer werden nicht Freunde.

old:

an ~ bag (pej.)	eine alte Schachtel
~ before one's time	schwächer, als das Lebensalter vermuten ließe
~ beyond one's years	reifer, als in dem Alter üblich
~ boy!	Alter Junge!
the ~ buffer	alter Mann
~ enough to be s.b.'s father/mother	alt genug sein, um jds. Vater/Mutter zu sein
an ~ flame	eine ehemalige Beziehung, eine alte Flamme
an ~ fogey	ein alter Kauz
~ hat	aus der Mode; ein alter Hut
an ~ maid	eine alte Jungfer
~, unhappy, far-off things	Sorgen der Vergangenheit

an ~ wives' tale	Legende, Märchen
the oldest profession	das horizontale Gewerbe
an olive branch	ein Friedensangebot
on:	
~ and off	gelegentlich
~ cloud nine (Sl.)	im siebten Himmel, sehr glücklich
~ edge	nervös
You can't have been sleeping well lately, you are so on edge.	
~ one's toes	aufmerksam
~ second thoughts	nach reiflicher Überlegung
~ the spur of the moment (Sl.)	Hals über Kopf, plötzlich
~ the face of it	offensichtlich, anscheinend
~ the got	beschäftigt
~ the one hand	einerseits
~ the verge of ...	kurz davor sein ...
~ the wrong track	auf der falschen Fährte
have had s.o. ~ about s.th. (Sl.)	jdn. wegen einer Sache gesprochen haben
have s.th. ~	etwas vorhaben
that's not ~	das kommt nicht in Frage
what's ~? (Sl.)	Was gibt es? Wie sieht es aus?
once:	
~ again	noch einmal
~ bitten, twice shy. (Sprichw.)	Gebranntes Kind scheut das Feuer.
~ and for all	ein für alle Mal
~ in a blue moon	alle Jubeljahre
~ in a while	gelegentlich
~ learnt, it isn't easily forgotten.	Was man einmal gelernt hat, vergisst man nicht so leicht.
~ too often	einmal zu viel
I tell you, you will be late once too often and then you will be out of a job!	
~ upon a time	es war einmal
give s.o. the ~-over (Sl.)	jdn. kurz betrachten

one:	
~ after the other	einer nach dem anderen
~ and all	jeder
~ day	eines Tages
~ for the road	ein letztes Glas vor dem Aufbruch
~ good turn deserves another. (Sprichw.)	Hilfts du mir, so helf ich dir. Eine Hand wäscht die andere.
~ of these days	irgendwann, gelegentlich
a ~-horse town	ein Kaff
~ in the eye for s.b.	ein Schlag ins Gesicht
~ in a million	einzigartig
a ~-man band	eine Einmannband
be ~ up on s.o. (Sl.)	jdm. voraus sein
~ man's loss is another man's gain. (Sprichw.)	Des einen Verlust ist des anderen Gewinn.
~ man's meat is another man's poison. (Sprichw.)	Was einem schadet, nützt dem anderen.
~ and only	absolut einzigartig
~ swallow does not make a summer. (Sprichw.)	Eine Schwalbe macht noch keinen Sommer.
~ thing and another	verschiedene Dinge/ Angelegenheiten
~ way or the other	auf die eine oder andere Weise
I for ~	ich zum Beispiel
~ on ~ (Sl.)	unter vier Augen
only:	
an ~ child	Einzelkind
~ fair	nur recht und billig
~ just	nur ganz knapp
~ too conscious of s.th.	man ist sich einer Sache nur zu sehr bewusst, man weiß etwas ganz genau
the onus is on ...	die Verantwortung liegt bei ...
ooh and aah	lauthals Begeisterung oder Erschrecken äußern

The people oohed and aahed when the clown entered the cirus.

open:	
~ and above board	offen und ehrlich

~ the floodgates	Tür und Tor öffnen
~ Pandora's box	die Büchse der Pandora öffnen, unbedacht Unheil verursachen
an ~ question	eine noch ungeklärte Frage
~ season for	Jagdsaison
~ up to s.o.	mit jdm. offen reden
the operative word	der springende Punkt
the opium of the people	Opium des Volkes, Religion
opposite number	Gegenstück
or:	
~ else	oder etwas Unangenehmes wird geschehen
~ I'm a Dutchman	ich bin mir absolut sicher
~ rather	oder um es genauer zu sagen
~ so	oder so, etwa
ordeal by fire	Prüfung der Standhaftigkeit (eigentlich: Gottesurteil)
the order of the day	1. Planung oder Programm für den Tag, 2. üblich
other:	
the ~ side of the coin	die Kehrseite der Medaille
~ things being equal	wenn sich die Lage ansonsten nicht ändert
every ~	jeder zweite
the ~ day	neulich
our man in	unser Vertreter an einem bestimmten Ort
out:	
~ cold	bewusstlos
The boxer knocked his opponent out cold.	
~ of all proportion	maßlos übertrieben, in keinem Verhältnis
~ and about	wieder auf den Beinen

I'm pleased to see you out and about after your illness.	
~ and ~	gänzlich
The girl is an out-and-out genius.	
~ for the count	bewusstlos
~ of date	altmodisch
~ of order	außer Betrieb, kaputt
~ of print	vergriffen
~ of the corner of one's eye	aus dem Augenwinkel
~ of the frying pan, into the fire	vom Regen in die Traufe
~ of the woods (Sl.)	nicht mehr in der kritischen Phase
be ~	nicht zu Hause sein
have it ~ with s.o.	sich mit jdm. aussprechen
pull ~	sich zurückziehen
take it ~ on s.b.	etwas an jdm. auslassen
the ins and ~s	die Einzelheiten
outstay one's welcome	länger bleiben, als dem Gastgeber lieb ist
over:	
all ~	aus und vorbei
~ and above s.th.	über etwas hinaus
~ and done with	aus und vorbei
~ my dead body!	Nur über meine Leiche!
~ one's head	zu hoch für jdn.
~ s.o. (Sl.)	über jdn. hinweg sein
overshoot the mark	über das Ziel hinausschießen
overstep the mark	eine Grenze überschreiten, übertreiben
owe s.b. a debt of gratitude	jdm. Dank schuldig sein
own:	
hold one's ~	sich behaupten
on one's ~	allein, selbstständig
~ up to s.th.	sich zu etwas/einer Tat bekennen
The boy owned up to having stolen the apples.	
get one's ~ back	sich rächen

P

pack:	
~ one's bags	sein Bündel schnüren, abreisen
~ it in! (Sl.)	Hör auf damit!
~ s.o. off somewhere	jdn. fortschicken, fortjagen
Mother packed the boys off to the beach so she could go shopping.	
~ed like sardines	wie die Heringe, sehr eng
We were packed like sardines in the coach to London.	
a ~ of lies	lauter Lügen
The story he told was nothing but a pack of lies.	
send s.o. ~ing	jdn. kurzfristig entlassen, jdn. abservieren, jdn. kurz abfertigen
paddle one's own canoe	auf eigenen Füßen stehen
pain:	
be a ~ in the neck (Sl.)	einem auf die Nerven gehen
take ~s to do s.th.	sich bei etwas große Mühe geben
He took great pains to help her settle in.	
paint:	
~ a gloomy picture of s.th.	ein düsteres Bild von etwas malen
~ the town red	die Stadt unsicher machen, feiern
beyond the pale	jenseits des Zumutbaren
palm s.th. off (Sl.)	jdm. etwas andrehen
a paper tiger	Papiertiger
par:	
~ excellence	ganz besonders

~ for the course (Am.)	typisch, was man erwarten konnte
His performance at tennis was quite par for the course.	
up to ~	dem erwarteten Niveau entsprechend
a paragon of virtue	ein Muster/Ausbund an Tugend (iron.)
the parish pump	Klatsch und Tratsch in einer ländlichen Gemeinde
Once he had retired, his interests in life revolved mostly around the parish pump.	
part:	
~ and parcel of s.th.	fester Bestandteil; samt und sonders
A glittering tree, presents and good food are all part and parcel of Christmas. *He packed his family off part and parcel to spend a holiday in the country.*	
for my ~	was mich betrifft
for the most ~	weitgehend, meistens
take in good ~	nicht beleidigt sein
take ~ in	teilnehmen an
take s.b.'s ~	Partei ergreifen für jdn.
~ with s.o. or s.th.	sich von jdm. oder etwas trennen
be partial to	mögen, gern haben
I am rather partial to roast beef and Yorkshire pudding.	
a party piece	ein besonderes Glanzstück
pass:	
~ away/on	sterben
~ a remark	eine Bemerkung machen
~ for	gelten als

~ judgement	ein Urteil fällen
~ off	1. vorgeben, dass, 2. einen falschen Eindruck erwecken, 3. langsam weniger werden
1. She disliked his bad manners, but tried to pass them off as a joke. *2. The girl liked to pass herself off as much older than she was.* *3. A feeling of nausea overcame her, but it soon passed off.*	
~ on	weitergeben
~ one's/the time	sich die Zeit vertreiben
~ out	ohnmächtig werden
~ over s.th./s.o.	über etwas/jdn. hinweggehen
~ the buck (Sl.)	jdm. den schwarzen Peter zuschieben
~ the time of day	jdm. Guten Tag sagen
past:	
not to put it ~ s.o.	jdm. etwas durchaus zutrauen
I wouldn't put it past John to take his girlfriend along on a business trip.	
~ caring	sich nicht mehr um etwas kümmern
patch:	
not to be a ~ on s.th. (Sl.)	sich nicht mit etwas messen können
to hit a bad ~ (Sl.)	eine Pechsträhne haben
Patience is a virtue. (Sprichw.)	Geduld ist eine Tugend.
pay:	
the devil to ~ (Brit./Sl.)	ein fürchterlicher Aufruhr
If you don't do as he says, there'll be the devil to pay.	
~ attention	aufmerksam zuhören
~ back	1. zurückzahlen, 2. heimzahlen
1. He paid back the money he owed. *2. I'll pay you back one day for the harm you have done me.*	

~ s.o. a visit	jdn. besuchen
~ through the nose for s.th. (Sl.)	einen Haufen Geld für etwas bezahlen
He who pays the piper calls the tune. (Sprichw.)	Wer die Musik bezahlt, bestimmt die Melodie.
the pearly gates	die Himmelstür
as like as two peas in a pod (Sl.)	sich gleichen wie ein Ei dem anderen
pecking order	Hierarchie, Hackordnung
a peeping Tom	ein Spanner
take s.o. down a peg or two (Sl.)	jdm. einen Dämpfer verpassen
pen:	
The ~ is mightier than the sword. (Sprichw.)	Die Feder ist mächtiger als das Schwert.
a ~ portrait	eine schriftliche Beschreibung
penny:	
a pound to a ~	wahrscheinlich
cost a pretty ~	eine hübsche Summe Geld kosten
in for a ~, in for a pound	wenn schon, denn schon
spend a ~ (Sl.)	die Toilette aufsuchen
perfidious Albion	die verräterischen Engländer
Perish the thought!	Gott bewahre!
a phoenix from the ashes	Phoenix aus der Asche
pick:	
~ a quarrel with s.b.	jdn. kritisieren, sticheln
~ and choose (Brit.)	vorsichtig aussuchen
~ on s.o./s.th.	kritisieren, herumnörgeln
~ holes in s.th./s.o.	etwas/jdn. kritisieren
~ one's way	seinen Weg suchen
~ one's words (Brit.)	sich vorsichtig ausdrücken

~ out — auswählen, herausfinden
~ o.s. up — wieder aufstehen, sich erheben, sich aufraffen
~ s.b.'s brains — Ideen übernehmen, jdn. aushorchen
~ s.b. up — jdn. abholen, treffen
~ s.th. up — etwas aufschnappen
~ up (Sl.) — sich erholen

be in a pickle (Brit./Sl.) — in der Patsche sitzen

it's no picnic — Das ist kein Honigschlecken.

picture:
see ~s in the fire — in die Flammen schauen
put s.o. in the ~ — jdn. ins Bild setzen über, jdn. einweisen

Let me put you in the picture: the train will be late due to mechanical problems at the next station.

that's all ~s in the sky — das sind nur verrückte Ideen

piece:
a ~ of cake — ganz einfach, keine Herausforderung
be of a ~ with s.th. — genau zu etwas passen
give s.o. a ~ of one's mind (Brit./Sl.) — jdm. den Kopf waschen, jdm. gründlich die Meinung sagen

pig:
~ in the middle — zwischen zwei Stühlen
buy a ~ in a poke (Brit./Sl.) — die Katze im Sack kaufen
happy as a ~ in muck — rundum zufrieden

pile:
make one's ~ (Brit./Sl.) — einen Haufen Geld verdienen
~ it on (thick) — übertreiben
~s of s.th. (Sl.) — haufenweise
~ up — sich anhäufen
My work is piling up, I must spend more time on it.

pillar:

a ~ of society	eine Stütze der Gesellschaft
from ~ to post	von Pontius zu Pilatus

pin:

~ down	festnageln, festmachen
~ money	Taschengeld
~ s.o. down to s.th.	jdn. auf etwas festnageln
~ s.o.'s ears back (Am./Sl.)	jdn. schelten, schlagen
~ up	anstecken, feststecken

see pink elephants	weiße Mäuse sehen

pipe:

~ down!	Red' nicht so viel!
put that in your ~ and smoke it (Sl.)	Das kannst du dir hinter die Ohren schreiben.
~ up	dazwischenreden, unterbrechen

piping hot	kochend heiß

pitch and toss	Kopf oder Zahl, hin- und herschaukeln

pity:

What a ~!	Schade!
take ~ on	Mitleid empfinden für, jdm. helfen

place:

be going ~s (Sl.)	es zu etwas bringen, Erfolg haben
do a ~ up (Sl.)	renovieren
in the first ~	erstens, zuallererst
in ~ of	an Stelle von
out of ~	fehl am Platz, nicht geeignet
put o.s. in s.b.'s ~	sich in die Lage von jdm. versetzen

plain:

as ~ as the nose on your face (Sl.)	sonnenklar
~ dealing	offenes, ehrliches Handeln

~ speaking	Klartext reden
~ sailing	eine klare Sache
be ~ with s.b.	mit jdm. offen reden
play:	
~ ball	kooperieren
bring s.th. into ~	etwas ins Spiel bringen
~ fast and loose with s.o. (Sl.)	mit jdm. (emotional) spielen
It was really not okay to play fast and loose with her feelings like that.	
~ for time	Zeit herausschinden
~ the game	die Regeln einhalten, ehrlich spielen
~ hooky (Am./Sl.)/~ **truant** (Brit.)	die Schule schwänzen
~ it cool	ruhig bleiben
~ it safe	kein Risiko eingehen
~ into s.o.'s hands	jdm. in die Hände spielen
~ one's cards well	die Gelegenheit ausnutzen
~ s.th. down	etwas herunterspielen
~ with fire	ein Risiko eingehen, mit dem Feuer spielen
~ed out	erschöpft, ausgebrannt
plead guilty	sich schuldig bekennen
Please God	wenn Gott will
plenty of s.th.	reichlich
plight one's troth	sich die Treue schwören
plough a lone furrow	allein auf weiter Flur stehen
give s.th. a plug (Sl.)	für etwas werben
pocket:	
have long ~s and short arms (Sl.)	geizig sein
put one's pride in one's ~	über seinen Schatten springen, klein beigeben
in one's ~	in der Tasche, unter Kontrolle
be out of ~	finanzielle Verluste erleiden

point:	
be on the ~ of doing s.th.	kurz davor sein, etwas zu tun
make a ~ of s.th.	auf etwas Wert legen
He made a point of welcoming the late-comers very warmly.	
~ out	hinweisen auf, hervorheben
stick to the ~	bei der Sache bleiben, nicht abschweifen
come to the ~	auf den Punkt kommen
That's not the ~.	Darum geht es nicht.
The ~ is that ...	Die Sache ist die, dass ...
make a ~	zur Diskussion beitragen
not to put too fine a ~ on it	das Kind beim Namen nennen, nicht um etwas herumreden, etwas Wichtiges sagen
a sore ~	ein wunder Punkt
My going out to work is a sore point with my husband.	
stretch a ~	ein Zugeständnis machen
The librarian will stretch a point and let me have the book for another week.	
strong ~	Stärke
Cleaning the house is not my strong point.	
take s.o.'s ~	die Meinung von jdm. akzeptieren
~ of view	Meinung, Standpunkt
a poison-pen letter	anonymer Brief
poke:	
~ fun at	sich lustig machen über
~ one's nose into s.th.	seine Nase in etwas stecken
pop:	
~ down	mal schnell hingehen
I will just pop down to the shops for some biscuits.	
~ in	hereinplatzen, auf einen Sprung vorbeikommen
My neighbour is always popping in for a cup of tea.	
~ the question (Sl.)	einen Heiratsantrag machen

keep s.o. posted (Sl.)	jdn. auf dem Laufenden halten
postpone the evil hour/day	ein unerfreuliches Ereignis vor sich herschieben
pot:	
The ~ calls the kettle back. (Sl.)	Ein Esel schilt den anderen Langohr.
go to ~ (Sl.) *If you don't paint your fence soon it'll go to pot.*	ganz kaputt gehen
pour:	
It never rains but it ~s.	Ein Unglück kommt selten allein.
~ forth	darauflosreden
~ cold water on s.th.	dämpfend wirken
~ oil on troubled water	beruhigen, schlichten, die Wogen glätten
power:	
be the ~ behind the throne	die graue Eminenz sein
the ~'s that be	„die da oben", die Mächtigen
a practical joke	ein Streich
Practice makes perfect. (Sprichw.)	Übung macht den Meister.
practise what one preaches	seine Lehren auch in die Tat umsetzen
precious few/little	nur sehr wenige/wenig
a pregnant silence	beredtes Schweigen
present company excluded	das Gesagte gilt nicht für die Anwesenden
press:	
be ~ed for *I can't stop and talk to you now, I'm pressed for time.*	kaum genug haben
~ for	pochen auf, bestehen auf
~ forward/on with	vorankommen mit

I want to press on with the work on our book.

Prevention is better than cure. (Sprichw.)	Vorbeugen ist besser als heilen.
prick up one's ears	die Ohren spitzen
in the prime of life	in den besten Jahren
the primrose path	der Rosenpfad
small print	das Kleingedruckte
private:	
one's ~ life	Privatleben
a ~ eye (Sl.)	ein Privatdetektiv
Procrastination is a thief of time. (Sprichw.)	Aufschieb ist ein Tagedieb.
the prodigal son	der verlorene Sohn
promise the moon	das Blaue vom Himmel versprechen
proof:	
The ~ of the pudding is in the eating. (Brit. Sprichw.)	Probieren geht über Studieren.
put to the ~	testen
prop s.th. up	etwas stützen (besonders: im finanziellen Sinne)
a proper Charlie	dumm, unfähig
prophet:	
~ of doom	ein Schwarzseher
The ~ is without honour in his own country. (Sprichw.)	Der Prophet gilt nirgends weniger als im eigenen Land.
pros and cons	die wesentlichen Argumente dafür und dagegen; Pro und Kontra

Before bringing the meeting to a close, Robert once again reviewed the pros and cons and asked for a decision.

be proud of s.th.	stolz auf etwas sein
prove one's case	eine Behauptung beweisen
prunes and prisms	übermäßig korrekte Aussprache
You pseud!	Du Angeber!
a pub crawl (Sl.)	Kneipentour
puff and blow	vor physischer Erschöpfung pusten und schnaufen
a puffing billy	Dampflokomotive
pull:	
~ **a fast one over s.o.**	jdn. reinlegen
~ **a long face** (Brit.)	ein langes Gesicht machen
~ **o.s. together**	sich zusammennehmen, zusammenreißen
~ **rank**	seine Position zu seinem eigenen Vorteil nutzen
~ **s.th. off** (Sl.)	etwas erreichen, schaffen
~ **s.o.'s leg**	jdm. einen Bären aufbinden, jdn. zum Besten halten
~ **s.o.'s socks up**	sich zusammenreißen
~ **strings**	die Fäden aus dem Hintergrund ziehen, Beziehungen spielen lassen

It's easy to get a job if you have a rich uncle to pull strings.

~ **the wool over s.o.'s eyes**	jdn. hinters Licht führen
~ **one's weight**	seinen Teil leisten
pure and simple	schlicht, genau so
push:	
~ **home**	nach Hause eilen

~ **s.o.** (Sl.)	jdn. unter Druck setzen
~**ing up the daisies** (Sl.)	die Radieschen von unten wachsen sehen, tot sein

put:

~ **a spoke in s.o.'s wheel**	jdm. Knüppel zwischen die Beine werfen
~ **about**	1. besorgt, ängstlich, 2. in Umlauf bringen

1. I was quite put about when I didn't hear from you.
2. The news of his arrival was immediately put about.

~ **above all else**	vor alles andere stellen
~ **an end to s.th.**	einer Sache ein Ende bereiten
~ **by**	zurücklegen, beiseite legen, auf die hohe Kante legen
~ **in a (good) word for**	ein (gutes) Wort einlegen für
~ **in an appearance**	erscheinen, auftauchen
~ **ideas into s.o.'s head**	jdm. Flausen in den Kopf setzen
~ **in order**	in Ordnung bringen
~ **into the shade**	in den Schatten stellen
~ **into force**	in Kraft setzen
~ **into words**	in Worte fassen
~ **it down to ignorance**	etwas auf Unwissenheit zurückführen, als Dummheit auslegen
~ **off one's stride**	aus dem Tritt gebracht
~ **on the shelf**	an den Nagel hängen
~ **on one's thinking cap**	scharf nachdenken
~ **on weight**	zunehmen (Gewicht)
~ **one's finger on s.th.**	den Kern der Sache treffen
~ **one foot before the other**	einen Fuß vor den anderen setzen
~ **one's oar in** (Sl.)	seinen Senf dazugeben
~ **one's heads together** (Sl.)	die Köpfe zusammenstecken
~ **o.s. forward**	sich hervortun
~ **o.s. in s.b.'s place**	sich in jdn. hineinversetzen
~ **out of action**	außer Gefecht setzen
~ **pressure on**	Druck ausüben auf
~ **s.b. off**	1. aus der Fassung bringen, 2. jdm. absagen

1. Your always being late really puts me off.

2. I've got to go to the doctor this afternoon so I've had to put John off.	
~ s.b. on his guard	jdn. warnen
~ s.th. on the scrap heap (Sl.)	etwas ausrangieren
~ s.b. through it	jdn. auf Herz und Nieren prüfen
~ s.o. down	jdn. fertig machen
~ s.o. through the hoop(s)	jdn. einer schweren Prüfung unterziehen
~ s.th. right	etwas richtig stellen
~ s.b. on the spot	jdn. in Verlegenheit bringen
~ s.b. up	jdn. beherbergen
~ s.o. wise to s.th.	jdn. über etwas informieren, jdm. Bescheid geben
~ the lid on s.th.	etwas die Krone aufsetzen
~ the blame on s.b.	jdm. die Schuld in die Schuhe schieben
~ the cart before the horse	das Pferd von hinten aufzäumen
~ the kibosh on s.th. (Sl.)	etwas ein jähes Ende bereiten
~ two and two together	sich einen Reim machen auf, zwei und zwei zusammen zählen
~ up with s.th.	sich etwas gefallen lassen
~ word into s.o.'s mouth	für jdn. ohne dessen Erlaubnis sprechen
a Pyrrhic victory	ein Pyrrhussieg

Q

quarter:

live in close ~s	eng beeinander wohnen
in all ~s	überall
Queen Anne is dead.	Das ist nichts Neues. Jeder weiß das.

queer:

a ~ card	ein Exzentriker
The man had lived on his own quite happily for years but was obviously a queer card.	
~ s.b.'s pitch	jdm. einen Strich durch die Rechnung machen
I must see my bank manager about a loan quickly, if my boss talks to him first it might queer my pitch.	

question:

the ~ of the hour	das Thema, das momentan am meisten beschäftigt
be out of the ~	außer Frage stehen, nicht in Frage kommen
beg the ~	auf eine Frage ausweichend reagieren, sich vor einer Entscheidung drücken
beyond all ~	ohne Frage, zweifellos
no ~s asked	keine dummen Fragen stellen
The ~ does not arise.	Die Frage stellt sich nicht.
quibble about s.th.	sich über Kleinigkeiten streiten

quick:

~ on the draw	schlagfertig
~ on the uptake	von rascher Auffassungsgabe
a ~ one	ein schnelles Glas zwischendurch
cut to the ~	tief betroffen, verletzt
I was cut to the quick when my fiancé broke off our engagement.	

a quid pro quo	etwas beruht auf Gegenseitigkeit
quiet:	
on the ~	insgeheim, unter der Hand
~ down	sich beruhigen
quite:	
~ so!	Ganz recht so!
~ a bit	ziemlich viel
~ a few	ziemlich viele
~ a number	eine beträchtliche Zahl
~ a lot	ziemlich viel/viele

R

race:	
~ against time	Wettlauf mit der Zeit; gegen die Uhr arbeiten
rack:	
~ one's brains	sich den Kopf zerbrechen
on the ~	äußerst gespannt, auf glühenden Kohlen
(go to) ~ and ruin	verkommen, vor die Hunde gehen
His health is going to rack and ruin.	
rag:	
a ~ and bone man	Straßenhändler, Lumpenhändler
all the rage (Sl.)	der letzte Schrei
rain:	
come ~ or come shine	in jedem Fall
It's ~ing cats and dogs.	Es regnet Bindfäden. Es gießt wie aus Kübeln.
It never ~s but it pours.	Ein Unglück kommt selten allein.
save up for a ~y day	auf die hohe Kante legen
The ~ falls on the just and the unjust.	Tugend schützt nicht gegen alles.
raise:	
~ an objection (to)	einen Einwand erheben gegen
~ from the dead	jdn. von den Toten auferwecken
~ one's eyebrows	leicht schockiert sein
~ one's hat to s.o.	vor jdm. den Hut abnehmen, jdn. grüßen
~ one's voice against s.th.	seine Stimme gegen etwas erheben
~ to the surface	an die Oberfläche bringen
~ the devil with s.o. (Sl.)	jdn. fürchterlich beschimpfen
rant and roar	lauthals protestieren
a rare bird	selten

rat:	
~s desert a sinking ship. (Sprichw.)	Die Ratten verlassen das sinkende Schiff.
smell a ~	den Braten riechen
rate:	
at any ~	auf jeden Fall
to ~ s.o.	jdn. schätzen
a raving beauty	eine strahlende Schönheit
give s.o. a raw deal	jdn. schlecht behandeln
ray:	
a ~ of sunshine	eine Aufmunterung
a ~ of hope	ein Hoffnungsschimmer
reach:	
~ for the sky	hohe Ziele haben, nach den Sternen greifen
~ out for	greifen nach
out of ~	unerreichbar
within easy ~	leicht erreichbar
read:	
~ between the lines	zwischen den Zeilen lesen
~ into	hineinlesen
~ out	laut vorlesen
~ s.th. up	etwas nachlesen
~ s.o. like a book	jdn. sehr gut kennen
ready:	
~ for anything	zu allem bereit
~, steady, go	auf die Plätze, fertig, los
really and truely	ganz sicher
reap the benefits of s.th.	von etwas profitieren
red:	
see ~	rot sehen
be in the ~	Schulden haben, in den roten Zahlen sein

like a ~ rag to a bull	wie ein rotes Tuch ...
~-handed	auf frischer Tat
The burglar was caught red-handed as he left the house with the stolen goods.	
the ~-light district	Rotlichtbezirk
see the ~ light	eine Warnung vor Schwierigkeiten erhalten
~ in the face	verlegen
regard:	
as ~s me	was mich betrifft
have no ~ for	nicht berücksichtigen, keine Rücksicht nehmen
reign supreme	alles beherrschen
rein:	
give ~	die Zügel locker lassen
keep a tight ~ on	zügeln
My aunt is very strict and keeps at tight rein on her teenage son.	
take the ~s	die Führung übernehmen
When her husband died Mary took the reins of the familly business.	
relieve:	
~ one's feelings	seinen Gefühlen freien Lauf lassen
~ s.b. of his money	jdm. das Geld wegnehmen, beklauen, betrügen
be reluctant to	etwas widerwillig tun
remark:	
pass a ~ on	sich äußern über
The teacher passed a remark on the clothes his pupils were wearing.	
without ~	kommentarlos, stillschweigend
render a service	unterstützen, helfen

rest:	
~ upon s.th.	sich auf etwas stützen
set s.b.'s fears at ~	jdn. beschwichtigen
The doctor set my fears at rest when he told me I wasn't seriously ill.	
The responsibility ~s with you.	Du trägst die Verantwortung.
~ assured	beruhigt sein
~ on one's laurels	sich auf seinen Lorbeeren ausruhen
Revenge is sweet. (Sprichw.)	Rache ist süß.
There's neither rhyme nor reason in that.	Das hat weder Hand noch Fuß.
ride:	
~ a tiger	etwas Dummes oder Gefährliches tun
~ one's hobby-horse	seinem Steckenpferd/ Zeitvertreib nachgehen
~ roughshod	ohne Rücksicht weitermachen
The young man rode roughshod over his parents' arguments and refused to take their advice.	
take s.o. for a ~	jdn. auf die Schippe nehmen
right:	
put to ~	berichtigen
You are ~ to do so.	Du hast Recht, dich so zu verhalten.
~ away	sofort
The lawyer said he would see his client right away.	
by ~s	rechtens, nach dem Recht
serve s.o ~	jdm. recht geschehen
It serves you right if you are wet, you shouldn't have started splashing me.	
~ as rain	auf dem Damm, in Ordnung
The doctor said I was as right as rain and could go back to school.	

ring:	
~ a bell with s.o.	jdm. bekannt vorkommen
give s.o. a ~	jdn. anrufen
~ s.b. up	jdn. anrufen
run ~s round s.o.	jdm. weit überlegen sein
~ with	widerhallen von
The hall rang with the happy laughter of the children at the party.	
~ off	ein Telefonat beenden
He was obviously offended, as he rang off without saying a word.	
rip s.o. off (Sl.)	jdn. übers Ohr hauen
rise:	
~ and shine!	Aufwachen!
~ to the occasion	sich der Situation gewachsen zeigen
risk:	
at one's own ~	auf eigene Gefahr
run a ~	ein Risiko eingehen
~ one's neck	Kopf und Kragen riskieren
roll:	
~ up one's sleeves	die Ärmel hochkrempeln
Tears ~ down her cheeks.	Tränen laufen ihr die Wangen herunter.
The years ~ by.	Die Jahre vergehen.
room:	
~ for improvement	verbesserungsfähig, nicht ganz einwandfrei
~ and to spare	viel Platz
~ with s.o.	mit jdm. eine Wohnung/Zimmer teilen
root:	
~ and branch	komplett, vollständig
the ~ of the trouble	die Wurzel des Übels

rope:	
~ s.o. into (doing) s.th.	jdm. eine Arbeit aufhalsen
My brother roped me into helping him to move about the furniture.	
know the ~s	die Spielregeln kennen
rose:	
see life through ~-tinted spectacles	das Leben durch die rosarote Brille sehen
~s all the way	uneingeschränkt angenehm
rough:	
it is ~ on s.o.	es ist hart für jdn.
~ it	primitiv leben
When we go on holiday we don't stay in hotels, we like to rough it.	
have a ~ time	eine schwere Zeit haben
take the ~ with the smooth	es nehmen, wie es kommt
round:	
a long way ~	ein Umweg
go ~ to s.b.'s	jdn. besuchen
I'm going round to Mary's for the evening.	
~ off	vollenden, fertig machen
~ on	jdm. die Schuld geben, beschimpfen
He rounded on his servant for losing the cases.	
rub:	
~ it in (Sl.)	jdm. unter die Nase reiben
~ s.o. up the wrong way	jdn. verärgern
~ shoulders with s.o.	mit jdm. in Kontakt kommen
rude health	stabile Gesundheit
rue the day	ein Ereignis bereuen
ruffle s.b.'s feathers	jdn. verärgern
rule:	
as a ~	im Allgemeinen, generell

~ out	ausschließen
~ing passion	persönliche Vorliebe, Lieblingszeitvertreib
Her ruling passion was to tend to her garden.	

run:

~ a temperature	Fieber haben
~ across	zufällig begegnen
~ up against s.th.	auf etwas stoßen
~ aground	(Schiff) auf Grund laufen
~ away with the idea	sich einbilden
~ counter to	im Widerspruch stehen zu
This completely runs counter to our plans.	
five days ~ning	fünf Tage nacheinander
give s.o. a ~ for his money (Sl.)	jdn. fordern, Leistung abverlangen
James thought it would be easy beating Harold at squash, but he gave him a run for his money.	
in the long ~	langfristig
in the short ~	kurzfristig
on the ~	auf der Flucht
~ out of ...	keine ... mehr haben
May I borrow some milk? I've run out and want to bake a cake.	
~ s.o. over	jdn. überfahren
~ short of s.th.	knapp werden
We are running short of time, you have to hurry up.	
~ner-up	der Zweite
Even though Jim won the race, Bill was the runner-up.	
up and ~ning	in Betrieb, funktionierend
~-off	Wettkampf
give s.o. the run-down (Sl.)	jdn. über etwas informieren
Jack will give you the run-down on what happened in London last week.	

rush:

~ one's fences	etwas übers Knie brechen
~ headlong	überstürzen
~ into doing s.th.	etwas überstürzt tun
~ s.o. to hospital	jdn. schnellstens ins Krankenhaus bringen

in a rut — in eingefahrenen Gleisen

What I am really afraid of in my job is to get into a rut.

S

get the sack (Brit./Sl.)	entlassen werden
a sacred cow *I would have liked to say something about the company uniform, but had been told in advance that it was a holy cow, so I kept my mouth shut.*	heilige Kuh
saddle s.o. with s.th.	jdm. etwas aufbürden
safe:	
a ~ bet	eine sichere Sache
a ~ job	ein sicherer Arbeitsplatz
be on the ~ side	auf der sicheren Seite sein
play it ~	auf Nummer sicher gehen
~ and sound	gesund und munter
when all is said and done	unterm Strich, letzten Endes
sail close to the wind	sich an der Grenze des Zulässigen bewegen
sake:	
for ...'s ~	um ... willen, aus Liebe zu ...
For God's ~!	Um Gottes willen!
one's salad days	unschuldige Jugendjahre
salt:	
~ away	auf die hohe Kante legen
not worth one's ~ *Her kitchen equipment was really not worth its salt.*	nichts taugen
~ of the earth	absolut integer
with a pinch of ~	mit Vorbehalt nehmen, nicht für bare Münze nehmen

same:	
the ~ again?	Nochmal das Gleiche?
same here (Sl.)	das sehe ich genauso
the ~ old story	eine bekannte Geschichte
the ~ the world over	es ist überall das Gleiche
What's sauce for the goose is sauce for the gander.	Was dem einen recht, ist dem anderen billig.
save:	
~ one's breath	den Mund halten
You may as well save your breath, the children aren't listening.	
~ s.b. from s.th.	jdn. vor etwas retten
~ the situation	die Lage retten
~ money	Geld sparen
~ up for (s.th.)	aufheben für, sparen für
~ s.o.'s bacon	jdm. die nackte Haut retten
say:	
~ cheese	Bitte lächeln!
have little to ~ for oneself	nichts zu seiner Rechtfertigung vorbringen können
have no ~ in s.th.	in einer Angelegenheit nichts zu sagen haben
not able to ~ boo to a goose	ängstlich sein
no sooner said than done	gesagt, getan
~ one's piece	seine Meinung sagen
That goes without ~ing.	Das versteht sich von selbst.
that is to ~	das heißt, vielmehr
when all is said and done	letzten Endes, unterm Strich
~ s.th. in a roundabout way	etwas umständlich zum Ausdruck bringen
~ s.th. to s.o.'s face	jdm. etwas ins Gesicht sagen
make o.s. scarce	sich aus dem Staub machen
scare:	
be ~d stiff	zu Tode erschrocken sein, eine Heidenangst haben
~ the living daylights out of s.o.	jdn. fürchterlich erschrecken
~ s.o. to death	jdn. zu Tode erschrecken

not my scene	nicht mein Geschmack
throw s.o. off the scent	jdm. Sand in die Augen streuen
scoop the pool	den Jackpot gewinnen
score:	
on that ~	in dieser Hinsicht
settle an old ~	eine alte Rechnung begleichen
scrape:	
get into a ~	in Schwierigkeiten geraten
~ the barrel	den letzten Rest auskratzen
~ acquaintance (with)	sich um eine Bekanntschaft bemühen
scratch:	
~ the surface of s.th.	sich nur oberflächlich mit etwas auseinandersetzen
~ one's head	sich am Kopf kratzen
up to ~	den Anforderungen entsprechen
start from ~	ganz von vorne anfangen
scream blue murder	laut Protest schreien
screw:	
put the ~ on s.b.	jdm. die Macht zeigen, jdn. zwingen
~ up one's courage	allen Mut zusammennehmen
~ up	etwas vermasseln
Scrub that! (Sl.)	Vergiss das!
the scum of the earth	wertloses Pack
seal s.b.'s fate	jds. Schicksal besiegeln
search:	
~ me! (Sl.)	Was weiß ich! Frag' mich etwas Leichteres!
in ~ of	auf der Suche nach
~ after	streben nach
make a ~ for	suchen nach

second:

~ nature to s.o.	einfach/selbstverständlich für jdn.
~ to none	besser als alle(s) andere(n)
I ~ that	ganz meine Meinung
on ~ thoughts	nach reiflicher Überlegung

see:

~ eye to eye with s.o. on s.th.	in einer Angelegenheit voll mit jdm. übereinstimmen
Morton and I see eye to eye on the matter of expanding into new markets.	
~ with half an eye	sofort/auf einen Blick sehen
~ how the land lies	sehen, wie der Hase läuft
~ s.th. done	dafür sorgen, dass etwas geschieht
~ about/to s.th.	sich kümmern um
~ s.o. across the street	jdn. über die Straße bringen
~ s.b. home	jdn. nach Hause bringen
~ s.o. off	jdn. verabschieden
~ s.b. through s.th.	jdm. in einer schwierigen Situation beistehen
~ s.th. through	etwas zu Ende führen
~ to it that	dafür sorgen, dass

seize:

be ~d with	ergriffen/befallen sein von (Anfall, fixe Idee etc.)
~ the opportunity	die Gelegenheit nutzen

s.o.'s usual self	wie immer
She was her usual happy self.	

sell:

~ the pass	jdn. verraten
~ at a loss	mit Verlust verkaufen
~ like hot cakes	sich wie warme Semmeln verkaufen
~ s.b. down the river	jdn. verraten
~ s.o. a pup	jdn. übers Ohr hauen

send:

~ a boy to do a man's work	jdn. mit einer Aufgabe betrauen, die ihn überfordert

~ s.b. crazy	jdn. aufregen/wahnsinnig machen
~ for s.th.	nach etwas schicken
~ s.b. packing	jdn. fortjagen
~ word to s.o.	jdm. eine Nachricht schicken
I'll send word that we'll be catching the later train.	

sense:

make ~	Sinn ergeben, sinnvoll sein
make ~ of s.th.	etwas verstehen/begreifen
talk ~	vernünftig sein/reden

serve:

~ as an excuse	als Entschuldigung dienen
~ its purpose	seinen Zweck erfüllen
That ~s them right.	Das geschieht ihnen recht.
at your service	zu Ihren Diensten

set:

~ a good example	ein gutes Beispiel abgeben
be hard ~	in großer Not sein
dead ~ against s.th.	absolut dagegen sein
~ a dog on s.b.	einen Hund auf jdn. hetzen
~-back	Rückschlag
~-to	ernsthafter Streit
They had a real set-to about whose job it was to do the dishes.	
~ fire to	anzünden
~ foot in	eintreten
~ great store by	große Stücke halten auf
~ in	beginnen, einsetzen
It looks as if winter will set in early this year.	
~ one's heart on	sich etwas von Herzen wünschen
~ one's mind to	sich etwas in den Kopf setzen
~ one's teeth on edge	durch Mark und Bein gehen
~ s.b. down	jdn. absetzen
~ to rights	in Ordnung bringen
~ to work	zu arbeiten beginnen
~ up (shop)	(ein Geschäft) etwas aufbauen/einsetzen/ins Leben rufen
The Prime Minister set up a committee to investigate the matter.	

settle:

~ back	sich zurücklehnen
~ down	sich niederlassen, sesshaft werden, sich beruhigen
~ on s.th.	sich für eine Sache entscheiden
She settled finally on the pink dress, not the blue.	
~ with s.o.	mit jdm. abrechnen
~ for s.th.	sich mit etwas zufrieden geben
~ up	die Zeche zahlen

seven:

the ~ deadly sins	die sieben Todsünden
~th heaven	der siebte Himmel, Paradies

all sewn up	alles unter Dach und Fach

shake:

~ one rigid	jdn. erschrecken
~ like a leaf	wie Espenlaub zittern
~ hands	sich die Hand geben
~ in one's shoes	vor Angst zittern
~ s.o. up (Sl.)	jdn. schockieren/aufregen

shall be nameless	jmd. oder etwas soll nicht namentlich erwähnt werden
Various members of our group, who shall be nameless, did not contribute as much as we had hoped.	

shame:

~ on you!	Schäm dich!
put s.o. to ~	jdn. in den Schatten stellen
What a ~!	Wie schade!

Shank's pony	zu Fuß

the shape of things to come	zukünftige Entwicklungen

share:

have a ~ in	teilhaben an, Anteil haben an
~ out among	verteilen unter

~ and ~ alike	zu gleichen Teilen (teilen)
sharp:	
~ practice	unsaubere Geschäfte
~en one's wits	seinen Geist schärfen
That was a close shave.	Das wäre beinahe ins Auge gegangen.
shed:	
~ blood	Blut vergießen
~ light on	Licht werfen auf
~ tears over	Tränen vergießen über
sheep:	
a wolf in ~'s clothing	ein Wolf im Schafspelz
cast ~'s eyes at	verliebt/schmachtend ansehen
have a sheet in the wind (Sl.) *Tom really had a sheet in the wind when he came back from the pub last night.*	einen in der Krone haben
shift:	
~ for s.b. *The boys had to shift for themselves when their mother was ill.*	alleine zurechtkommen
~ from one foot to the other	von einem Fuß auf den anderen treten
~ the responsibility on ...	die Verantwortung auf ... schieben
~ one's ground	die Meinung, den Standpunkt ändern
shine:	
a shining light	sehr gut, auffallend
a shining example	ein leuchtendes Beispiel
~ like a good deed in a naughty world	positiv hervorstechen
make a ~ about	Aufhebens machen um
take the ~ out of	in den Schatten stellen
~ up to s.o. (Am.)	um die Gunst von jdm. bitten
shipshape and Bristol-fashion	in bester Ordnung

keep one's shirt on	ruhig bleiben
It gives me the shivers.	Es läuft mir kalt den Rücken herunter.
get the shock of one's life	einen Schock fürs Leben bekommen
shoe:	
know where the shoe pinches	wissen, wo der Schuh drückt
be in s.o.'s ~s	in der Haut von jdm. stecken
shoot:	
~ ahead	schnelle Fortschritte machen
~ a glance at	einen raschen Blick werfen auf
shop:	
all over the ~	überall
~ around	einen Einkaufsbummel machen
talk ~	fachsimpeln
short:	
fall ~ of s.th.	nicht den Erwartungen entsprechen
run ~ of	knapp werden, zur Neige gehen
~ of cash	knapp bei Kasse
two bricks ~ of a load (Sl.)	dämlich
just ~ of London	kurz vor London
cut s.o. ~	jdn. unterbrechen, jdm. über den Mund fahren
I was about to explain my reasons, but he cut me short.	
~-lived	von kurzer Dauer, kurzlebig
~ with s.o.	kurz angebunden
shot:	
~ in the dark	auf bloße Vermutung hin, ins Blaue hinein
~ in the arm	finanzielle Unterstützung
have a ~ at s.th.	etwas versuchen, ausprobieren
like a ~	blitzartig

straight from the shoulder	direkt, geradeheraus
shove off (Sl.) *Just shove off and leave me alone, will you?*	sich verziehen
show:	
~ a clean pair of heels	schneller sein als jmd. anderes
~ off	angeben, prahlen
~ one's hand	mit offenen Karten spielen
~ one's mettle	seinen Mut unter Beweis stellen
~ up	aufkreuzen
~ promise	vielversprechend wirken
run the ~	den Laden schmeißen
a shrinking violet	Mimose, Feigling
shrug one's shoulders	mit den Achseln zucken
shudder to think ...	man mag sich gar nicht vorstellen, dass ...
shut:	
~ down	(endgültig) schließen
~ one's eyes to s.th.	die Augen vor etwas verschließen
~ up! (Sl.)	Halt den Mund!
~ the stable door when the horse has bolted	den Brunnen zudecken, wenn das Kind schon ertrunken ist
sick:	
~ at heart	unglücklich
~ of the sight of s.th. or s.b.	jdn. oder etwas nicht mehr sehen können
I'm ~ and tired of it.	Das hängt mir zum Hals raus.
side: ~	
a bit on the ... ~	ein wenig ...
~ with s.b.	jdm. beistehen, für jdn. Partei ergreifen
~ against s.b.	gegen jdn. Partei ergreifen
~ by ~	nebeneinander, einträchtig
split one's ~s with laughter	vor Lachen umkommen

sight:
at first ~ auf den ersten Blick
lose one's ~ erblinden
~ for sore eyes ein willkommener Anblick
not by a long ~ bei weitem nicht

silence reigns es ist vollkommen still

the silver screen Kino, Filmbranche

sing:
~ a different song seine Meinung ändern
~ s.b.'s praises jdn. öffentlich loben

sink:
~ like a stone ein Schlag ins Wasser
~ into oblivion in Vergessenheit geraten, in der Versenkung verschwinden
~ into sleep in tiefen Schlaf fallen
It's ~ or swim. Vogel friss oder stirb.
~ing sand Treibsand

sit:
~ back and do nothing die Hände in den Schoß legen
~ on the fence zwischen zwei Stühlen sitzen
~ s.th. out bis zum Ende bleiben, etwas aussitzen
~ tight (Sl.) ausharren, geduldig warten
~ up for s.b. für jdn. aufbleiben, auf jdn. warten
a ~ting duck ein leichtes Ziel
~ting pretty es gut haben

six:
~ of one and half a dozen of the other Jacke wie Hose, gehupft wie gesprungen
at ~es and sevens durcheinander, konfus

the sixty-four thousand dollar question die alles entscheidende Frage

a skeleton in the cupboard eine Leiche im Keller

skin:	
~ and bone	Haut und Knochen
by the ~ of one's teeth	mit Hängen und Würgen, mit knapper Not
save one's ~	seine eigene Haut retten
the sky's the limit	nach oben sind keine Grenzen gesetzt
slap-bang in the middle of	genau in der Mitte von
a slap-up meal	ein großes Essen
sleep:	
~ rough	draußen schlafen
~ like a log	schlafen wie ein Murmeltier
~ tight	Gute Nacht!
not to ~ a wink	kein Auge zumachen
up one's sleeve	in der Hinterhand
sleight of hand	Fingerfertigkeit
slice:	
a ~ of life	ein Ausschnitt aus dem Leben
a ~ of luck	eine Portion Glück
slip:	
~ away	entwischen
~ into	hineinschlüpfen, sich hineinstehlen
~ s.th. on/over	sich etwas überziehen
~ through one's fingers	durch die Finger schlüpfen/ rutschen
~ of the tongue	Versprecher
Freudian ~	Freud'scher Versprecher
give s.o. the ~	jdm. entkommen
~ up	Fehler machen
be on the slippery slope	auf der schiefen Bahn sein
the slough of despond	eine Phase der Verzweiflung
slow:	
my watch is ~	meine Uhr geht nach

~ly but surely	langsam aber sicher
~ on the uptake	schwer von Begriff
small:	
~ beer/potatoes	bedeutungslos
the ~ change of s.th.	die unwesentlichen Aspekte von etwas
the ~ print	das Kleingedruckte
the ~ screen	Fernseher
~ talk	(höfliche) Konversation
a smart alec	Klugscheißer
smell a rat	Lunte riechen
smoke:	
~ like a chimney	viel rauchen, wie ein Schlot rauchen
a ~ screen	Tarnung, Täuschung
smooth:	
~ s.b.'s path	jdm. den Weg ebnen
a ~ customer	ein ganz gerissener Kerl
That's the snag.	Da liegt der Hase im Pfeffer.
snap:	
a cold ~	eine Kältewelle
a ~ vote	eine vorschnelle Entscheidung
~ at s.b.	jdn. barsch anfahren
~ out of (Sl.)	abwerfen, loswerden, sich aus etwas zurückziehen
I wish he would snap out of his present mood.	
a snare and a delusion	etwas erscheint sicher, ist aber nicht so
not to be sneezed at	nicht zu verachten
so:	
~ far, ~ good	so weit so gut, bis jetzt ist alles in Ordnung

~ help me God	so wahr mir Gott helfe
~ long (Sl.)	auf Wiedersehen
~ many words	nur Gerede
~ much the better	um so besser
~ there!	Aha!
~ what? (Sl.)	Na und?

sober:

~ facts	ungeschminkte Tatsachen
a ~ing truth	eine ernüchternde Wahrheit

soft:

~ in the head	schwachsinnig
a ~ job	eine leichte Arbeit
a ~ option	eine Entscheidung für den einfacheren Weg
~ pedal s.th.	sehr zurückhaltend und diskret vorgehen
~ soap	Schmeichelei

be sold down the river — verraten und verkauft

sole and heel — Schuhe reparieren
The gentleman has been soling and heeling in that little shop of his for as long as I can remember.

some time or other — gelegentlich

someone or other — einer von, jemand

something:

~ doing (Sl.)	etwas passiert
~ else again	eine ganz andere Sache
~ like (Sl.)	genau das, was man will
~ out of the ordinary	ungewöhnlich

somewhere, over the rainbow — im Reich der Fantasie

song:

for a ~	für 'n Appel und 'n Ei
make a ~ about	Aufhebens machen um

sooner:	
~ or later	früher oder später, irgendwann
~ you than me	es ist mir lieber, es betrifft dich, als mich
soothe the savage beast	Ärger oder Aufruhr besänftigen
a sore point	ein kritisches Thema, ein wunder Punkt
sorry:	
~ for oneself	selbstmitleidig
in a ~ state	in einem beklagenswerten Zustand
sort:	
~ s.th. out	1. etwas in Ordnung bringen, 2. jdn. zurechtweisen
1. He sorted out his problems. *2. If you don't get this done, I will come over and sort you out!*	
~ed for s.th. (Sl.)	ausgestattet für
out of ~s	schlecht gelaunt
be the soul of politeness	die Freundlichkeit in Person sein
Susan is the soul of politeness, I have never heard her utter an evil word to anybody.	
sound:	
~ and fury	leerer Schall, lautstarke Aktivität
~ in wind and limb	gesund und munter
~ the death knell of s.th.	einer Sache den Todesstoß versetzen
The invention of television was widely regarded as sounding the death knell of radio.	
be in the soup	in der Patsche sitzen
sow:	
~ the dragon's teeth	Zwietracht säen
~ one's wild oats	sich die Hörner abstoßen

call a spade a spade	das Kind beim Namen nennen
throw a spanner in the works	jmd. einen Knüppel zwischen die Beine werfen
spare:	
~ no expense	keine Ausgaben scheuen
one's ~ time	Freizeit
speak:	
~ the same language	sich über etwas gut verständigen können, dieselbe Sprache sprechen
~ of the devil (and he appears).	Wenn man vom Teufel spricht, kommt er.
generally/roughly ~ing	im Großen und Ganzen, grob gesagt
not to ~ of	ganz zu schweigen von
nothing to ~ of	nichts Erwähnenswertes
so to ~	sozusagen
~ volumes	Bände sprechen
~ one's mind	seine Meinung sagen
~ up	lauter reden
~ up for s.o.	jdn. verteidigen, für jdn. sprechen
spead the parting guest	jdn. formell verabschieden
spend:	
~ one's force	seine Kraft erschöpfen
~ money as if it's going out of fashion	Geld mit vollen Händen ausgeben
~ money as like water	mit Geld um sich werfen
spick and span	tipptopp, geschniegelt und gebügelt
spike s.b.'s guns	jdm. den Wind aus den Segeln nehmen
spill the beans (Sl.)	ein Geheimnis verraten
cry over spilt milk	über Dinge jammern, die nicht mehr zu ändern sind

spin:	
in a flat ~	in Panik
~ a yarn	Seemannsgarn spinnen, eine erfundene Geschichte erzählen
~ out	in die Länge ziehen
The spirit is willing but the flesh is weak. (Sprichw.)	Der Geist ist willig, aber das Fleisch ist schwach.
spit:	
be the ~ting image of s.o.	jdm. wie aus dem Gesicht geschnitten sein
~ it out!	Spuck's aus! Sag es endlich!
put a spoke in s.o.'s wheel	jdm. einen Knüppel zwischen die Beine werfen
sponge off s.o.	jdm. auf der Tasche liegen
be born with a silver spoon in one's mouth	reich auf die Welt kommen, mit einem goldenen Löffel im Mund geboren sein
spot:	
a ~ of	etwas von, ein wenig
a soft ~ for	eine Schwäche für
be on the ~	zur Stelle sein
~ on	ganz genau
knock the ~s off s.o.	jdn. in die Pfanne hauen
spread:	
a good ~	eine üppige Mahlzeit
~ like a wildfire	sich wie ein Lauffeuer verbreiten
spring clean	aufräumen, sauber machen
square:	
~ the circle	das Unmögliche möglich machen
a ~ peg in a round hole	am falschen Ort zur falschen Zeit, absolut nicht passen
a stag party	Junggesellenabschied

stage:

~ and screen	Theater und Kino
~ a strike	einen Streik ausrufen

be at stake	auf dem Spiel stehen

stamp:

a man of that ~	ein Mann dieses Schlages
set one's ~ on	seinen Stempel aufdrücken

stand:

make a ~	Widerstand leisten
not to ~ for s.th	etwas nicht dulden
~ a chance	eine Chance haben
~ by	bereitstehen
~ corrected	seinen Fehler eingestehen, sich verbessern lassen
Frank stood corrected when Dan looked it up in the book.	
~ for	repräsentieren, stehen für
~ in for s.o.	jdn. vertreten
~ in good stead	jdm. nützlich sein
~ on ceremony	sehr förmlich sein
~ out	hervorragen
~ together	zusammenhalten
~ up for	eintreten für
~ s.o. up	jdn. sitzen lassen
~ well with s.o.	mit jdm. gut stehen
~ for s.th.	etwas dulden
I will not stand for this kind of treatment.	
as it ~s	so, wie es im Moment aussieht
It ~s to reason.	Es ist ganz klar und logisch.

on standby	in Bereitschaft
the star turn	die Hauptattraktion
s.th. stares s.o. in the face	etwas ist für jdn. nicht zu übersehen
stark mad	vollkommen verrückt

start:

~ a hare	ein Thema anreißen, eine Diskussion starten
~ to rot	anfangen zu verrotten
to ~ with	zunächst einmal
That gave him a ~.	Das ließ ihn zusammenzucken/zusammenfahren.

state:

a ~ of affairs	die Umstände
a ~ of grace	Zustand der Seligkeit
the ~ of play	der Spielstand, die Lage bis jetzt

stay:

a ~ of execution	ein Aufschub der Hinrichtung
~ the course	bis zum Ende weitermachen
~ put	1. sich nicht bewegen, 2. halten

1. Stay put while I look for John.
2. This car just won't stay put, it breaks down once a week.

Steady on!	Vorsichtig!, Langsam!

Steady on, the two of you, you are going to hurt yourselves!

steal:

~ away	sich davonstehlen
~ the show/scene	jdm. die Show stehlen
~ s.b.'s thunder	jdm. den Applaus, die Lorbeeren stehlen

steer:

~ clear of	vermeiden, umgehen
~ a middle course	eine gemäßigte Position einnehmen

stem:

~ the flow	die Flut eindämmen
~ the tide	eine Bedrohung abwenden, zurückdrängen

step:

~ in	einschreiten, unterbrechen

~ on it (Sl.)	einen Zahn zulegen, sich beeilen
~ on the gas	Gas geben, sich beeilen
~ out of line	aus der Reihe tanzen

stick:

~ around	herumlungern
~ to the point	bei der Sache bleiben
get hold of the wrong end of the ~	auf dem Holzweg sein
~ by s.o.	jdm. treu bleiben, unterstützen
~ one's neck out (Sl.)	seinen Kopf riskieren
~ s.th. out	etwas aushalten
~ up for s.o.	jdn. unterstützen
My brother always stuck up for me at school when we were young.	
the ~ing point	die Grenze

be a stickler for s.th.	es mit etwas peinlich genau nehmen

Still waters run deep. (Sprichw.)	Stille Wasser sind tief.

stink:

~ like a polecat	stinken wie die Pest
~ing rich	stinken vor Geld

stint:

do a ~ on s.th.	zeitweise an etwas arbeiten
~ on s.th.	mit etwas geizen

stir one's blood	jdn. aufrütteln, jds. Herz höher schlagen lassen

A stitch in time saves nine. (Sprichw.)	Was du heute kannst besorgen, das verschiebe nicht auf morgen.

stock:

one's ~ is high/low	jds. Aktien steigen/fallen (fig.)
Stolen sweets are sweetest. (Sprichw.)	Je strenger das Verbot, je süßer schmecken die Äpfel.

a stone's throw of	nur einen Katzensprung/ Steinwurf entfernt

stop:

~ dead	plötzlich stehen bleiben
~ short	vor etwas anhalten
~ off	Zwischenstation einlegen
We are going to stop off in Salzburg on the way to Vienna.	
~ behind	da bleiben
~ by (Am./Sl.)	vorbeischauen

store:

be in ~ for s.b.	jdm. bevorstehen
set great ~ by	Wert legen auf

a storm in a teacup	ein Sturm im Wasserglas

story:

the ~ goes	man erzählt sich
cut a long ~ short	kurz gesagt

Stout fellow! (Sl.)	Tapferer Kerl!

straight:

give it to s.o. ~	mit jdm. ohne Umschweife reden
keep a ~ face	ernst bleiben
~ ahead	geradeaus
~ answer	eine direkte Antwort
~ away/off	sofort
~ from the shoulder	direkt, geradeheraus
~ up (Sl.)	Ehrlich!
~-forward	schlicht, einfach, geradeheraus

strain:

~ at a gnat and swallow a camel. (Sprichw.)	Mücken seihen und Kamele verschlucken.
~ed relations	gespannte Beziehungen

a stranger in a strange land	nicht vertraut mit seiner Umgebung

straw:

a ~ in the wind	ein Vorzeichen
the ~ that breaks the camel's back	der Tropfen, der das Fass zum Überlaufen bringt

That's the last ~.	Das ist der Gipfel.
clutch catch/grasp at (a) ~(s)	sich an einen Strohhalm klammern
the stream of consciousness	Bewusstsein
street:	
~s ahead of s.b./s.th.	viel besser als
right up one's ~	genau nach jds. Geschmack
strengthen s.b.'s hand	jds. Position verbessern
stresses and strains	Belastungen
stretch:	
~ a point	großzügig verfahren
~ one's legs	sich die Beine vertreten
strictly speaking	genau genommen
strike:	
~ a bargain	sich geschäftlich einig werden
~ home	tief treffen
~ at the root of	an der Wurzel treffen
~ a happy medium	zu einem Kompromiss kommen
be struck all of a heap (Sl.)	da vergeht einem Hören und Sehen
~ s.o. as	jdm. als ... erscheinen
~ while the iron is hot	das Eisen schmieden, solange es heiß ist
~ up a conversation	ins Gespräch kommen
have s.o. on a string	jdn. am Gängelband haben
a stroke of good luck	Glücksfall
strong:	
~ language	Kraftausdrücke
~ meat	starker Tobak
a ~ point	eine Stärke
protest in ~ terms	energisch protestieren
stuck for s.th.	etwas fehlt jdm.

I seem to be stuck for change, can you lend me a pound?

stuff:	
made of the same ~	aus dem gleichen Holz geschnitzt sein
know one's ~	auf Draht sein
~ and nonsense!	Unsinn!
a ~ed shirt (Sl.)	ein aufgeblasener Kerl
a stumbling block	Stolperstein
subject:	
~ to this	unter diesem Vorbehalt
~ to change	Änderungen vorbehalten
sore ~	wunder Punkt
such:	
~ is life.	So ist das Leben.
no ~ thing	nichts dergleichen
a sucker for s.th.	man kann etwas nicht widerstehen

I know it's expensive, but I have always been a sucker for fast cars.

not to suffer fools gladly	keine Geduld mit dummen Leuten haben
suffice it to say	es genügt zu sagen, dass ...
sufficient:	
~ unto oneself	selbstständig
~ unto the day	man soll sich nicht vorab Sorgen machen
a sugar daddy (Sl.)	ein älterer Mann, der ein junges Mädchen aushält
Suit yourself.	Mach, wie du meinst.
the sum total	das Endergebnis
Sunday:	
one's ~ best	die besten Kleider

a month of ~s	lange Zeit
sure:	
~ enough	genau, wie erwartet
a ~-fire method	eine ganz sichere Sache
~ of oneself	sehr selbstbewusst
~ thing! (Sl.)	Natürlich! Sicher!
surprise:	
~, ~	(iron.) Überraschung!
a ~ packet (Sl.)	Überraschung
swallow:	
~ the dictionary	ungewöhnliche Worte benutzen
~ one's pride	seinen Stolz hinunterschlucken, über seinen Schatten springen
He had to swallow his pride and admit he was wrong.	
~ the pill (Sl.)	in den sauren Apfel beißen
~ s.th. hook, line and sinker (Sl.)	etwas ohne weiteres glauben
~ an insult	eine Beleidigung hinnehmen
swear:	
~ black is white	eine unhaltbare Position energisch verteidigen
~ blind that (Sl.)	bekräftigen
~ at s.b.	auf jdn. fluchen
~ by s.th.	auf etwas schwören
~ in	vereidigen
sweat:	
~ blood (Sl.)	Blut schwitzen
be in a cold ~ (Sl.)	Blut und Wasser schwitzen
sweep:	
~ the board	alle nur möglichen Preise gewinnen
make a clean ~	reinen Tisch machen
~ across one's mind	einem in den Sinn kommen
~ s.o. off his feet	jdn. umhauen (fig.)
sweet:	
~ Fanny Adams	unwesentlich, wertlos

~ tooth	Naschkatze
keep s.o. ~	jdn. bei Laune halten
in full swing *The party was in full swing by the time we got there.*	voll im Gange
be switched on (Sl.)	auf Draht sein

T

T:

cross the ~'s	sehr genau/pedantisch sein
to a ~	aufs Haar, ganz genau
This description is correct to a T.	
keep tabs on s.o.	jdn. kontrollieren
be on the wrong track	auf dem Holzweg sein

tail:

~ after s.b.	jdm. hinterherlaufen
~ between his legs	wie ein erschrockener Hund, mit eingezogenem Schwanz
~-end Charlie	langsam, zu spät
turn ~ on s.b.	vor jdm. davonlaufen
~ off	schwächer werden
~ wagging the dog	das Unwichtige maßgebend sein lassen
~s up	in guter Stimmung

take:

~ advantage of s.b./s.th.	jdn./etwas ausnutzen
~n with s.th.	von etwas eingenommen sein
~n aback	überrascht
I was quite taken aback when I opened the door and saw my long-lost uncle.	
~ after s.o.	jdm. ähneln
~ the air	einen Spaziergang machen
~ a back seat (Sl.)	jdm. den Vortritt lassen, die Kontrolle aus der Hand geben
~ a beating	Prügel beziehen
~ the bull by the horns (Brit.)	den Stier bei den Hörnern packen
~ exception to s.th.	an einer Sache etwas auszusetzen haben
~ a fancy to s.b.	sich vernarren in, eine Vorliebe entwickeln für

~ in for a ride	betrogen, auf die Schippe genommen
~ for granted	als Tatsache hinnehmen, voraussetzen
~ s.o. for granted	jdn. nicht genügend beachten
~ in good/bad part	in guter/schlechter Laune etwas hinnehmen
He usually takes my advice in good part.	
~ heart	sich ein Herz fassen
~ hold of s.th.	etwas ergreifen
~ in	irreführen, betrügen
We were completely taken in by his story.	
~ it from me	Sie können mir glauben
~ a joke	Spaß verstehen
~ it or leave it	wie Sie wollen
~ liberties with	sich Freiheiten herausnehmen bei
~ a liking to s.o.	jdn. mögen
~ note of	notieren, festhalten
~ notice of	beachten
~ offence at	Anstoß nehmen an
~ one's hat off to s.b.	vor jdm. den Hut ziehen
~ one's leave	sich verabschieden
~ one's life in one's own hands	die Verantwortung für sich selbst übernehmen
~ one's life	Selbstmord begehen
~ s.b.'s life	jdn. töten
~ one's time	sich Zeit lassen
~ pity on	sich erbarmen, jdm. helfen
~ the plunge	den entscheidenden Schritt wagen
~ revenge	sich rächen
~ s.b. at his word	jdn. beim Wort nehmen
I hope you are serious about inviting me to stay for the weekend as I intend to take you at your word.	
~ s.b's breath away	jdm. den Atem verschlagen
She was so beautiful it took my breath away.	
~ s.o. down a peg or two	jdm. einen Dämpfer verpassen
~ s.o. for s.o.	jdn. mit jdm. verwechseln
~ s.th. amiss	etwas übel nehmen
~ s.th. at face value	etwas für bare Münze nehmen

~ s.th. in one's stride	etwas leicht schaffen
~ s.th. out on s.o.	etwas (Ärger etc.) an jdm. auslassen
~ s.b.'s mind off s.th.	jdn. von etwas ablenken
~ stock	Bilanz ziehen
~ the edge of	mildern, die Schärfe nehmen
~ things as they come	die Dinge auf sich zukommen lassen
~ to one's heels	die Beine in die Hand nehmen
~ s.b. to task for s.th.	jdn. zur Rede stellen
~ turns at	sich abwechseln mit
What do you ~ me for?	Wofür halten Sie mich denn?
That ~s the biscuit!	Jetzt schlägt's 13!

talk:

~ back	frech antworten
How many times have I told you that it is rude to talk back at your elders?	
~ big (Sl.)	angeben
~ down to s.o.	herablassend zu jdm. sprechen, sich einfach ausdrücken
The Prime Minister was very conscious of his office and tended to talk down to journalists and members of parliament.	
~ like a Dutch uncle	jdn. ermahnen, ernsthaft mit jdm. sprechen
~ shop	fachsimpeln
~ s.o. down	jdn. im Gespräch überzeugen, jdn. überreden
~ s.o. into doing s.th.	jdn. zu etwas überreden
~ s.o. out of s.th.	jdm. etwas ausreden
~ s.o.'s head off (Sl.)	zu viel reden
~ s.o. round	jdn. überreden
~ round s.th.	drumherum
~ until one is blue in the face (Sl.)	reden bis man schwarz wird/bis zur Erschöpfung reden

tall:

a ~ order	viel verlangt
a ~ story	ein Lügenmärchen

It takes two to tango.	Es gehören immer zwei dazu.
teach:	
~ s.b. to do s.th.	jdm. beibringen, etwas zu tun
You can't ~ an old dog new tricks.	Der Mensch ist ein Gewohnheitstier.
~ one's grandmother to suck eggs	jdm. mit mehr Erfahrung gute Ratschläge geben
team spirit	Teamgeist
tear:	
~ away from	sich losreißen
~ down	abreißen
~ into s.o/s.th.	jdn. auf das Schärfste kritisieren
~ one's hair	sich die Haare raufen, wütend sein
~ to pieces *The critics tore the performance of Hamlet to pieces.*	in Stücke reißen, verreißen
~ up by the roots	mit der Wurzel ausreißen, ausrotten
in the teeth of	entgegen, trotz
tell:	
~ a mile off	leicht erkennen können
~ all	ein umfassendes Geständnis ablegen
~ told	alles in allem
~ s.b. different	jdn. berichtigen
~ against s.th.	gegen etwas sprechen
~ apart	auseinander halten, unterscheiden
~ on s.o.	jdn. verraten/verpetzen
~ s.o. off	mit jdm. schimpfen
~ s.o. porkies (Sl.)	jdn. anschwindeln
~ s.o. where to get off (Sl.)	jdm. die Leviten lesen
~ tales	flunkern
temper:	
have a quick ~ *He has such a quick temper, every discussion ends in an argument.*	heftig sein, schnell in Wut geraten

keep one's ~	sich nicht aus der Ruhe bringen lassen
lose one's ~	die Beherrschung verlieren
tempt fate	das Schicksal herausfordern
ten:	
~ feet tall	sehr zufrieden mit sich selbst
~ to one	sehr wahrscheinlich
tend to	zu etwas neigen
These animals tend to get nervous during a thunderstorm.	
tender loving care	liebevolle Pflege
terms:	
be on bad ~ with	sich schlecht verstehen mit
come to ~ with	sich einigen mit, sich auf ... einstellen
in ~ of	hinsichtlich
not on speaking ~	zerstritten
on equal ~	zu gleichen Bedingungen, auf gleiche Weise
test:	
put to the ~	auf die Probe stellen
stand the ~	bestehen, sich bewähren
The old car stood the test and finished the race without breaking down.	
be at the end of one's tether	am Ende seiner Kräfte sein
He won't set the Thames on fire.	Der reißt keine Bäume aus.
thank:	
~ goodness/heaven	Gott sei Dank
~s to	dank, wegen
that:	
~ does it	das war es, mir reicht es, ich kann nicht mehr

~ is not to say	das soll nicht heißen
~ will be the day	das wird nie passieren
~ will do	das reicht
~'s all I can say	das ist alles

then:

~ and there	da und dort, auf der Stelle
~ again	andererseits

thick:

as ~ as two short planks (Brit./Sl.)	dumm wie Bohnenstroh
as ~ as thieves *They do simply everything together, they're as thick as thieves.*	wie Pech und Schwefel
a bit ~ (Brit./Sl.) *To expect me to pay all your bills is a bit thick.*	leicht unverschämt
come ~ and fast *After she had told her mother about her problems, the advice came thick and fast from all parts of the family.*	vor ... hageln, auf jdn. einstürmen
in the ~ of *We were suddenly caught up in the thick of the crowd.* *Don't keep me talking, please, I'm in the thick of a job.*	im dichtesten ..., mittendrin
~-skinned *He's too thick-skinned to see what everybody thinks of him.*	dickfellig
through ~ and thin	durch dick und dünn

thing:

a good ~ *It is a good thing you are wearing your coat, as the weather is just turning nasty.*	zum Glück, gute Sache
have a ~ about (Brit./Sl.)	besessen sein von
just one of those ~s	da kann man nichts machen, das ist nicht zu ändern
just the ~/the very ~	genau das Richtige
the ~ about s.th. is ...	die Sache ist die, dass ...

think:	
~ better of s.th.	einen schon gefassten Entschluss ändern
He thought better of his plan to go away and stayed at home.	
~ fit	beschließen, für angemessen erachten
The young man, having neither a job nor any money, thought fit to get married.	
~ highly of	bewundern, viel von jdm. halten
~ the world of s.o.	jdn. vergöttern, jdn. bewundern
put on one's ~ing cap	scharf über etwas nachdenken
He's a thorn in my side/flesh.	Er ist mir ein Dorn im Auge.
thought:	
A penny for your ~s!	Woran denkst du?
not to give s.th. another ~	keine Ursache
Thank you!	
Don't give it another thought!	
on second ~s	nach reiflicher Überlegung
On second thoughts, I think I'd prefer to fly.	
thread:	
lose the ~	den Faden verlieren
The professor lost the thread in the middle of his lecture.	
pick up the ~	den Faden wieder aufnehmen
It is difficult to pick up the thread in a discussion after an interruption.	
take s.o. through s.th.	jdm. etwas erklären
throw:	
~ away	durch Nachlässigkeit verlieren/wegwerfen
He threw away his chances of getting the job.	
~ in	hinzufügen, einwerfen
~ light on	Licht werfen auf
~ open	eröffnen, aufreißen (Tür)

~ one's money about	mit Geld um sich werfen
~ s.b. into work	sich in die Arbeit stürzen
~ o.s. at s.o.	sich jdm. an den Hals werfen
~ a spanner in the works	ein Hindernis in den Weg legen, eine Sache hintertreiben
~ s.o. off balance	jdn. aus dem Gleichgewicht bringen
~ s.o. over	jdm. den Laufpass geben
~ up	sich übergeben
under s.o.'s thumb	unter der Fuchtel von jdm.
thunderstruck	wie vom Blitz getroffen
a tissue of lies	von A bis Z erfunden
tick:	
in a ~	gleich, sofort
make s.o. ~ (Sl.)	jdn. motivieren
~ s.o. off	mit jdm. schimpfen
tickle:	
~ s.b.'s ribs	jdn. amüsieren
~d to death (Sl.)	äußerst amüsiert
~ s.o.'s fancy	jdn. interessieren, neugierig machen
the tide turns	die Dinge verändern sich
a tidy sum	eine ordentliche Menge Geld
tied up	ausgebucht, beschäftigt
tight:	
a little ~	in finanziellen Schwierigkeiten
in a ~ corner	in der Klemme
~-fisted	geizig
tighten one's belt	den Gürtel enger schnallen
time:	
ahead of ~	früher als erwartet
The expedition reached its destination well ahead of time.	

before one's ~	vor jds. Zeit, bevor man geboren wurde
for the ~ being	vorläufig
from ~ to ~	dann und wann
once upon a ~	Es war einmal ...
pressed for ~	sehr unter Zeitdruck
race against ~	Wettlauf gegen die Zeit
~ after ~	immer wieder
~ and ~ again	immer und immer wieder
~ of one's life	eine sehr schöne Zeit
It was a great holiday we had the time of our lives.	
have ~ on one's hands	Zeit zur Verfügung haben
to make good ~ (Am.)	gut vorankommen
give tit for tat	Gleiches mit Gleichem vergelten
today of all days	ausgerechnet heute
toe:	
~ the line	sich den Regeln/dem Druck beugen
The Prime Minister expects her cabinet to toe the line.	
keep s.o. on their toes	jdn. nicht zur Ruhe kommen lassen
tread on s.o.'s ~s	jdm. auf den Schlips treten
put heads together	gemeinsam überlegen
tongue:	
hold one's ~	den Mund halten, schweigen
get one's ~ around s.th.	etwas aussprechen
lose one's ~	kein Wort herausbringen
be on the tip of one's ~	auf der Zunge liegen
~ in cheek	ironisch
long in the tooth	alt
over the top	übertrieben
touch:	
get in ~ with	sich in Verbindung setzen mit
~ one's hat at s.o.	jdn. grüßen

~ and go	riskant
~ wood	auf Holz klopfen

track:

cover one's ~s	seine Spuren verwischen
off the ~	auf dem Holzweg
keep to the beaten ~	nichts Originelles wagen
make ~s	sich auf den Weg machen
off the beaten ~	abseits viel befahrener/ besuchter Routen

There weren't any tourists there at all, it was completely off the beaten track.

treat:

It is my ~.	Das geht auf meine Rechnung.
~ s.b. to s.th.	jdm. etwas spendieren, mit etwas verwöhnen

Grandma took the children to the park and treated them to an ice-cream.

trial and error	Versuch und Irrtum

trick:

be up to every ~	mit allen Wassern gewaschen sein
do the ~	den gewünschten Zweck erfüllen
not stick at trifles	sich nicht mit Kleinigkeiten abgeben

trouble:

ask/look for ~	Ärger suchen
take the ~	sich die Mühe machen
have no truck with s.th. (Sl.)	mit einer Sache nichts zu tun haben

true:

come ~	sich bewahrheiten
be ~ of	zutreffen auf
be ~ to s.b.	jdm. treu sein

show one's ~ colours	sein wahres Gesicht zeigen
come up trumps	eine Sache oder ein Problem zur allgemeinen Zufriedenheit lösen
try:	
~ one's hand at	sich in etwas versuchen, seinen ersten Versuch machen
John tried his hand at cooking while Mary was away.	
~ s.o.'s patience	die Geduld von jdm. auf die Probe stellen
sing another tune	einen anderen Ton anschlagen
turn:	
~ a deaf ear to	sich taub stellen
~ against s.o.	sich gegen jdn. stellen
not to ~ a hair	unbewegt bleiben, nicht mit der Wimper zucken
~ down	ablehnen
~ in	ins Bett gehen
~ inside out	das Innere nach außen kehren
~ one's back on s.b.	jdm. den Rücken zuwenden, sich von jdm. abwenden
He turned his back on me to indicate his displeasure.	
~ one's hand to s.th.	sich einer Sache zuwenden
~ out to be	sich herausstellen als/dass ...
~ over a new leaf	ein neues Leben beginnen, von vorn anfangen
~ s.b.'s brain/head	jdm. den Kopf verdrehen
~ s.o. in	jdn. bei der Polizei anzeigen/ verraten
~ s.th. over in one's mind	sich etwas im Kopf herumgehen lassen
~ s.th. upside down	das Unterste zuoberst kehren
~ tail	weglaufen, davonlaufen
~ the tables	den Spieß umdrehen
The arrival of the police on the scene turned the tables.	
~ to one's advantage	etwas zu seinem Vorteil wenden
~ up	aufkreuzen, erscheinen

~ tail — abhauen

~ upon s.b. — jdm. die Schuld geben, jdn. angreifen

The boy turned on his mother and said it was all her fault.

twiddle one's thumbs — Däumchen drehen, Zeit verschwenden

Don't just sit there twiddling your thumbs, get on with your work.

twig s.th. (Sl.) — etwas herausfinden, etwas merken

Jennifer finally twigged that Frank had been lying to her for absolute ages.

twist:

~ s.o.'s arms — jdn. unter Druck setzen

I had to twist his arm a little, but he finally came out with the full story.

~ s.o. round one's little finger — jdn. um den kleinen Finger wickeln

It takes two to tango. — Es gehören immer zwei dazu.

U/V

U speech	Sprechweise der Oberklasse
ugly:	
an ~ duckling	ein hässliches Entlein
as ~ as sin	hässlich wie die Nacht
the unacceptable face of s.th.	Aspekt einer Sache, den man auf keinen Fall tolerieren kann
unaware:	
be ~ of s.th.	sich einer Sache nicht bewusst sein, etwas nicht merken
catch s.o. ~	jdn. überraschen
under:	
come ~	klassifiziert werden als
~ the aegis of	unterstützt durch
~ cover of	im Schutz von
~ foot	am Boden
~ the guise of s.th.	in Verkleidung
~ s.b.'s nose	offen, in Gegenwart von jdm.
~ his own name	unter seinem eigenen Namen
~ one's own steam	mit eigener Kraft
~ par	nicht gut, unwohl
~ protest	etwas tun, aber sich zugleich dagegen verwahren
~ construction	im Bau befindlich
~ the counter	illegal, unter der Hand
~ the weather (Sl.) *John isn't coming to work today, he is feeling under the weather.*	unpässlich, krank
unfit for	ungeeignet zu, nicht fähig zu
Unity is strength.	Einigkeit macht stark.
United we stand (divided we fall). (Sprichw.)	Nur gemeinsam sind wir stark.

unwept, unhonoured and unsung	von niemandem beachtet oder vermisst
an unwritten law	ein ungeschriebenes Gesetz
up:	
~ in arms	empört
She was up in arms about the way everybody had been treating her.	
~ and coming	auf dem Weg zum Erfolg
~ and down the country	überall im Land
~s and downs	Höhen und Tiefen
~ and about	(wieder) gesund und munter
Mary was ill for a while, but now she is up and about again.	
~ against s.th.	in Schwierigkeiten stecken, vor einem Problem stehen
be ~ to s.th.	einen Plan aushecken
~ to it	in der Lage sein, etwas zu tun
You can't expect him to do that, he is simply not up to it.	
~ to no good (Sl.)	etwas im Schilde führen
~ hill and down dale	in allen Ecken des Landes
~ to scratch (Sl.)	den Erwartungen/Anforderungen gewachsen
John wants to compete in the tournament, but he is not really up to scratch.	
~ a tree (Sl.)	verzweifelt
Poor Gillian is up a tree after she lost everything in that fire.	
~ with s.th.	1. los sein mit jdm., 2. sich auskennen mit etwas
1. What's up with John? He certainly looks unhappy. *2. Is Henry up with the new technology they installed last week?*	
not ~ to much	nicht viel taugen
It's ~ to you.	Das liegt bei dir.
~ to par	durchschnittlich
upfront:	
be ~ about s.th.	offen über eine Sache reden

want s.th. ~ (Sl.)	einen Vorschuss haben wollen
upon my soul	ich schwöre es
the upper crust	die Aristokratie
upset:	
~ over s.th.	ärgerlich über etwas sein
~ s.th. (Sl.)	eine Sache durcheinanderbringen
upset s.b.'s applecart	jdm. in die Quere kommen
quick on the uptake	schnell kapieren
use:	
make ~ of	verwenden, ausnutzen
~ one's head	den Verstand gebrauchen
~ s.th. up	etwas aufbrauchen
~d to s.th.	an etwas gewöhnt sein
It's no ~.	Es hat keinen Zweck.
about as useful as	(iron.) so nützlich wie
vain:	
in ~	vergeblich
take in ~	leichtfertig mit etwas umgehen
Did someone take my name in ~?	Habe ich eben meinen Namen gehört? Hat da jemand von mir gesprochen?
the valley of the shadow of death	im finstren Tal
vanish into thin air	sich in Luft auflösen
variations of the theme *His letters were generally variations of the theme of his earlier complaints.*	Abwandlungen eines Motivs
Variety is the spice of life. (Sprichw.)	Abwechslung macht das Leben erst interessant.
with velvet gloves	sanft, mit Samthandschuhen

verge:	
be on the ~ of doing s.th.	im Begriff sein, etwas zu tun
be on the ~ of madness	am Rande des Wahnsinns stehen
this very	ganz genau, ausgerechnet
I shall complain to the police this very minute of you don't switch off the radio.	
the vexed question	die viel diskutierte Frage
a vicious circle	ein Teufelskreis, Circulus vitiosus
view:	
bird's-eye ~	Vogelperspektive
in my ~	meiner Meinung nach
in ~ of	angesichts
take a dim ~ of s.th.	etwas missbilligen
take a long ~	langfristig planen
the villain of the piece	der Bösewicht
virtue:	
~ is its own reward. (Sprichw.)	Die Tugend trägt ihren Lohn in sich selbst.
by ~ of	aufgrund, infolge
have the ~ of	den Vorteil besitzen, zu
The sofa has the virtue of being convertible into a bed.	
make a ~ of necessity	aus der Not eine Tugend machen
one's vital statistics	jds. physische Werte wie Größe, Gewicht etc.
voice:	
the ~ of conscience	die Stimme des Gewissens
at the top of one's ~	so laut wie möglich
give ~ to	zum Ausdruck bringen
raise one's ~	lauter werden, schreien
Don't raise your voice at me, I will not stand it!	
the ~ of reason	die Stimme der Vernunft
with one ~	einstimmig

W

the wages of sin	der Sünde Lohn, die gerechte Strafe
waifs and strays	obdachlose Kinder
go on the waggon (Sl.)	unter die Abstinenzler gehen
wait:	
~ for it	abwarten
keep s.b. ~ing	jdn. warten lassen
lie in ~	auf der Lauer liegen
~ and see	abwarten
~ on s.b.	jdn. bedienen
~ until the cows come home	lange warten, warten bis man schwarz wird
If he expects me to give up, he can wait until the cows come home!	
wake the dead	Tote wecken, Krach machen
walk:	
~ all over s.o.	jdn. sehr schlecht behandeln
~ off with	sich davonmachen mit
~ on air	glücklich sein
~ out on s.b.	jdn. verlassen/im Stich lassen
~ the plank	umgebracht werden
~ a tightrope	einen Balanceakt vollführen
~ of life	Beruf, sozialer Hintergrund
One of the benefits of this job is the opportunity to meet people from all walks of life.	
wall:	
~s have ears	die Wände haben Ohren, jmd. hört zu
~-to-~	viel von etwas
The place was covered in wall-to-wall greenery, it looked like a jungle to me.	

a Walter Mitty	ein Möchtegern-Held
a wandering Jew	eine rastlose Person
want:	
for ~ of	mangels
~ s.th. badly	etwas unbedingt wollen
~ out of s.th.	von etwas zurücktreten
war:	
a ~ of nerves	ein Nervenkrieg
~ to the knife	Kampf bis zum bitteren Ende
be at ~ with	auf Kriegsfuß stehen mit
be in the ~s	angeschlagen sein, mitgenommen aussehen
warm the chockles of s.b.'s heart	jdn. erfreuen und beruhigen
the warp and woof	Kette und Schuss
warts and all	mit allen seinen/ihren Fehlern
wash:	
~ one's hands of s.th.	seine Hände in Unschuld waschen
~-out	komplettes Versagen, Desaster
I tried to make a living as an artist, but it was a wash-out.	
waste:	
~ not, want not. (Sprichw.)	Spare in der Zeit, dann hast du in der Not.
~ away	dahinsiechen
~ s.b.'s time	jds. Zeit verschwenden
~ one's breath	Zeit verschwenden, umsonst reden
watch:	
~ every penny	sparsam sein
~ s.th. like a hawk	etwas genau beobachten
~ this space	pass genau auf (gleich passiert etwas)
~ it!	Aufpassen!

water:

be in low ~	auf dem Trockenen sitzen
fish in troubled ~s	im Trüben fischen
hold ~ *His account of the robbery won't hold water.*	schlüssig sein
in hot ~	in Schwierigkeiten
make s.b.'s mouth ~	jdm. den Mund wässrig machen
Still ~s run deep. (Sprichw.)	Stille Wasser sind tief.

way:

by the ~	übrigens
get into the ~ of *You will soon get into the way of using the computer.*	sich angewöhnen zu
go out of one's ~ to do s.th.	sich große Mühe geben, etwas zu tun
have one's ~	seinen Willen durchsetzen
pave the ~ for	den Weg bereiten für

wear:

~ s.b. out	jdn. erschöpfen, auslaugen
~ s.th. down/out	abnutzen, verbrauchen
~ on *The evening wore on and the guests were getting restless.*	sich dahinschleppen
~ the trousers	in einer Beziehung die Hosen anhaben
~ and tear	Abnutzung

weather:

feel under the ~	sich gesundheitlich nicht wohl fühlen
the ~ breaks/holds	das Wetter schlägt um/hält sich
~ the storm *The financial crisis plunged the company into severe difficulties, but they were able to weather the storm.*	Schwierigkeiten überstehen

weave one's spell	jdn. verzaubern

weigh:

~ anchor	den Anker lichten

~ the consequences	die Folgen abschätzen
~ the evidence	die Beweise abwägen
~ s.o. down	jdn. belasten, bedrücken
~ a ton	sehr schwer sein
~ on one's mind	jdn. beschäftigen, belasten
~ one's words	seine Worte abwägen, bedenken
~ up	einschätzen, beurteilen
He is a difficult person to weigh up.	
weight:	
take the ~ off one's feet	sich setzen
throw one's ~ about (Sl.)	sich aufspielen
you are welcome	bitte sehr, gern geschehen
well:	
~ I never!	Na so etwas!
~ met	was für ein glücklicher Zufall
~ and truly	gänzlich, gründlich
wet:	
~ the baby's head	aus Anlass einer Geburt einen trinken gehen
a ~ blanket	ein Spielverderber, ein Miesmacher
~ behind the ears	grün hinter den Ohren, unerfahren, unreif
~ one's whistle (Sl.)	etwas trinken
have a whale of a time	eine tolle Zeit haben
what:	
~ are we waiting for?	Worauf warten wir?
~'d you call him? (Sl.)	Wie heißt er doch gleich?
~ do you know!	Was für eine Überraschung!
and ~ have you	und so weiter
~ the eye doesn't see (the heart doesn't crave for). (Sprichw.)	Aus den Augen, aus dem Sinn.
I tell you ~.	Ich mach dir einen Vorschlag.
I tell you what: let's go to the cinema.	
so ~	na und, was macht das schon
~ a hope!	Schön wärs!
~ have you (Brit./Sl.)	Ähnliches, der Rest

Just put the suitcases and what have you in the boot.

whatever:

~ happened to ...?	Was ist aus ... geworden?
~ is, is right	die Dinge sind in Ordnung, wie sie sind
~ you do	unter allen Umständen

wheeling and dealing	Verhandlungen und Intrigen

wheels:

the ~ of government	die Mühlen der Regierung
~ within ~	komplizierte Arrangements

where:

~ does one go from here?	Wie geht es jetzt weiter?
~ on earth	wo auch immer
~ there's a will, there's a way. (Sprichw.)	Wo ein Wille ist, ist auch ein Weg.

which is not saying much	was nicht viel heißt

He was by far the best player in his team, which is not saying much.

a whiff of grapeshot	der begrenzte Einsatz von Feuerwaffen

have the whip hand	die Oberhand haben

white:

a ~-collar job	eine Schreibtischtätigkeit
a ~ elephant	nutzloser Gegenstand, Fehlinvestition
show the ~ feather	den Schwanz einziehen
tell a ~ lie	nicht ganz die Wahrheit sagen
a ~ night	eine schlaflose Nacht

who am I to argue	was rechtfertigt meinen Widerspruch

wild:

~ goose chase	ein sinnloses Unterfangen

~ guess	blinde Vermutung
~ horses wouldn't make me do it.	Keine zehn Pferde bringen mich dazu.
will:	
against s.o.'s ~	gegen den Willen von jdm.
Where there is a ~ there is a way.	Wo ein Wille ist, ist auch ein Weg.
win hands down	spielend gewinnen
wind:	
get ~ of	spitz kriegen, in Erfahrung bringen, von etwas Wind bekommen
get the ~ up (Sl.)	Angst haben
like the ~	schnell wie der Wind
put the ~ up s.o. (Sl.)	jdm. Angst einjagen
see which way the ~ blows	sehen, wie der Hase läuft
~ s.o. up (Sl.)	jdn. veralbern
take the ~ out of s.o.'s sails	jdm. den Wind aus den Segeln nehmen
wipe out (Sl.)	auslöschen, ruinieren
Many companies were wiped out when the stock index crashed.	
wise:	
get ~ to s.th. (Sl.)	etwas merken
put s.o. ~ to s.th. (Sl.)	jdm. etwas erklären, jdn. einweihen
Max finally put Jeremy wise to the tricks of his business.	
~ up to s.th. (Sl.)	den Tatsachen ins Gesicht sehen
wit:	
be at one's wit's ends	mit seinem Latein am Ende sein
keep one's ~s about one	seine fünf Sinne beisammen halten
out of one's ~s	von Sinnen
within:	
~ an ace of	beinahe
I was within an ace of being run down by the van.	

~ easy reach	leicht erreichbar
throw a wobbly (Sl.)	eine Szene machen
keep the wolf from the door	sich (finanziell) über Wasser halten
put the wool over s.o.'s eyes	jdm. Sand in die Augen streuen
word:	
have a quick ~ about s.th.	kurz über etwas reden
be as good as one's ~	sein Wort halten
be unable to get a ~ in edgewise	nicht zu Wort kommen
by ~ of mouth	mündlich
have the last ~	das letzte Wort haben
have ~s with s.o.	sich mit jdm. streiten
waste ~s	Worte verschwenden, vergeblich reden
~s fail me	ich bin sprachlos
work:	
make short ~ of	kurzen Prozess mit etwas machen, schnell beenden
~ upon	einwirken auf
~ one's way up	sich hocharbeiten
~ out	1. ausrechnen, 2. planen, 3. sich belaufen auf, 4. Sport treiben
1. The architect worked out how many apartments could be built on the site. *2. We'll work out the details of our holiday trip later.* *3. The cost works out at 5 pounds a head.* *4. He used to be overweight, but since he has taken to working out regularly, he has lost twenty kilograms.*	
~ wonders	Wunder wirken
for all the world	in jeder Hinsicht
worse for wear	abgenutzt, abgetragen

for what it's worth	ohne Gewähr
wrap:	
~ped up in	vollständig in Anspruch genommen von
He is wrapped up in his family.	
write:	
nothing to ~ home about	nichts besonderes
~ off	abschreiben, aufgeben
The goods are unsaleable, we had better write them off.	
hold the wrong end of the stick	etwas vollkommen falsch verstehen

Y/Z

year:	
~ in, ~ out	Jahr für Jahr; Jahr ein, Jahr aus
all the ~ round	das ganze Jahr über
not for donkey's ~s	seit Ewigkeiten
yearn for *When I was a kid I yearned for a little dog, but my parents would not allow it.*	sich sehnen nach
yell out *He yelled out when the horse trod on his foot.*	hinausschreien
not yet	noch nicht
yield:	
~ place to	Platz machen für
~ the right-of-way	jdm. die Vorfahrt lassen
~ to despair	sich der Verzweiflung hingeben
~ up s.th.	etwas aufgeben
zap (Sl.) *I'll just zap down to the supermarket and get some snacks.*	schnell irgendwohin flitzen
zero in on s.th.	etwas anpeilen, zielen auf
zip:	
~ along	schnell fahren
~ up	den Reißverschluss hochziehen

Register

A und O 20
ab und zu 8
Aber 121
abfinden 36
abgenutzt 238
abhauen 21
abkühlen 51
Abkürzung 56
abmachen 60
Abneigung 143
Abrakadabra 114
Abschied 138
Abschluss 54
absichtlich 36
abspülen 65
Abstinenzler 232
Abwesenheit 50
Ach und Krach 37
Achsel 200
Adamskostüm 25
adlig 27
Affäre 110
Ahnung 47, 69
Aktie 210
Akzent (haben) 6
Alarm 55, 119
Alkohol 69
allen Leuten Recht machen wollen 11
alles in allem 10, 19
allgemein 33
Allgemeinwissen 50
allmählich 36
Allüren 9
Alter 9, 61, 123
Amen 73
Anblick 110
andererseits 8
Anfang 16, 92
anfangen 75
Anfängerglück 22
angeben 28
Angeklagter 23
Angelegenheit 35
angeln 86
angeschrieben 26
Angesicht 78
Angst 89, 237
Anker 234
anrufen 38
anschließen 126
anschnauzen 28
anschwärzen 26
Ansehen 146
Ansicht 42, 120
anstellen 16
Anstoß 217
anstrengen 23
Antrieb 6
Anzahlung 40, 67
Apfel 44, 104, 210, 214
Applaus 33, 34, 96, 209
Arbeit 126, 150, 151, 189, 223
Ärger 41, 53, 225
Arm 35, 71
Arm in Arm 13
Ärmel 188
Armut 92
arrogant 114
Art 11
Ass 115
Ast 25, 131
Atem 217
Atemzug 32, 67, 135
attraktiv 80
auf allen vieren 10
auf Grund 6
aufatmen 5
aufbürden 18, 192
aufdonnern 99
aufdrängen 121
auffrischen 33
aufgeben 239
aufgehoben 81
aufgetakelt 88
Aufhebens 79, 93, 150, 198, 204

Aufmerksamkeit 41, 67
aufpassen 233
aufpeppen 125
aufregen 61
Aufruhr 171
Aufsehen 41
aufstöbern 63
Auge 12, 21, 27, 46, 55, 76, 77, 78, 122, 129, 130, 146, 150, 161, 166, 194, 198, 200, 202, 222, 235, 238
Augenweide 82
Augenwinkel 168
ausbaden 18
Ausbund 170
Ausdruck 231
Auseinandersetzung 20
ausführlich 16
aushalten 5, 39
auskommen 65
Ausnahme 76
ausnehmen 26
ausplaudern 21
Ausschau 146
Aussteuer 31
auswalzen 87
Ausweg 14

B 122
babyleicht 14
bagatellisieren 141
Bahn 202
Balanceakt 232
bald 22
Band 206
Bange 159
Bank 92
Bär 179
bar 40
Bau 228
Baum 161, 220
bedeuten 7
bedeutungslos 6
Bedingung 23, 50
Bedrohung 209
beeilen 110, 119
beeindruckend 114
beenden 33
befördern 131
Begeisterung 210
beglückwünschen 119
Begriff 118, 203
beharren 129
beherrschen 50
Beherrschung 28, 39, 88, 220
Bein 5, 67, 89, 104, 111, 113, 154, 167, 180, 196, 206, 207, 212, 218
Beispiel 196, 198
Belieben 17
bekannt 36
Belangloses 75
beliebt machen 13
Bemerkung 25, 139
Benehmen 5
benehmen 9
bereit 7, 11
Bereitschaft 208
bereuen 189
Berg 157
Bericht 6
berücksichtigen 21
berufen 151
Berufung 84
beruhigen 51
Berührung 110
Bescheidenheit 80
Bescherung 130
beschimpfen 38
Besen 110, 120, 159
Besitz 116
Besitzer 42, 107
Besserwisser 18
bestätigen 18
Beste(s) 20, 23
bestenfalls 23
besuchen 38
Betracht 11
betrifft 13, 14, 30
betrunken 106
Bett 115, 226
Beute 72
bewusst 10

Bewusstsein 26, 212
Beziehungen 50
Biegen 117
Biegen und Brechen 36
Bienchen 25
bienenfleißig 14
Bier 126
Bilanz 19, 218
Bild 169, 173
billig 193
Bindfaden 184
Binsen 67
bis jetzt 14
blank 109
Blatt 58, 153
blaublütig 27
Blaue 199
Blick 26, 57, 76, 78, 85, 99, 153, 195, 199, 201
blind 161
Blinder 27
Blitz 15, 20, 28, 29, 142, 223
blitzschnell 22, 27
Blödsinn 114, 118
Blumenkind 87
Blut 18, 27, 87, 198, 214
Boden 33, 94, 104, 111, 228
Bohnenstroh 15, 221
Bombe 19
Boot 29
bösartig 19
Bösewicht 231
Braten 185
brav 14
Brechen 117
Brei 21
Brennpunkt 118
Brieftasche 72
Brille 189
Brücke 34
Brunnen 200
brüten 162
Büchse 167
Bündel 169
Bürde 60
Busenfreund 30

Chance 42, 63, 97, 208
Chaos 50, 110

Dach 19, 107, 197
dahinschleppen 67
Damm 187
Dampf 28, 96, 139
Dämpfer 172, 217
Dank 168, 220
Däumchen 227
Daumen 54, 129
davonkommen 111
Decke 99, 101, 115, 149, 153
Deckel 120
Deckung 31
Definition 36
demütigen 73
denken 14
deprimiert 28
Detail 84, 127
Dichter 151
dichthalten 28
dick 82, 101, 221
Dienst 7, 196
Dinge 14
diskutieren 43
Distanz 13, 64
Doppelleben 137
Dorf 103
Dorn 222
Draht 19, 213, 215
drauf und dran sein 5
Dreck 64, 156
dreizehn 19, 218
Droge 117
Druck 180, 227
Drum und Dran 144
dulden 208
dumm 60, 75, 109, 112
Dummheit 114, 180
Dummkopf 104
Dunkeln 16
durchblättern 137
durchboxen 74
durchdrehen 101, 112
durchhalten 21, 52

Durchschnitt 6
Durst 74
Dutzend 37

Ecke 34, 68, 161
egal 39
Ehe 33, 152
Ehre 82, 98, 115
Ehrensache 117
Ehrenschulden 117
ehrgeizig 115
ehrlich 5, 117
Ehrlichkeit 117
Ei 89, 142, 172, 204
Eifer 113
Eile 119, 152
Eilschritt 17
Eimer 40, 67
Eindruck 53
einfach 14
einfallen 41
einhämmern 69
einholen 41, 94
Einkaufsbummel 199
einmischen 116
einnicken 69
einordnen 78
einstimmig 6, 36
einverstanden 79
Einwand 11
Einzelheiten 123, 168
Eis 32, 120
Eisen 112, 124, 212
Elefant 22, 34, 142, 150
Element 69
Elfenbeinturm 124
Eminenz 104, 177
Ende 11, 49, 67, 74, 111, 131, 181, 193
endlich 16
entlassen werden 85
Entlein 228
Entrüstung 119
Entscheidung 127
erblicken 41
Erfahrung 51, 137
Erfolg 24, 119, 127, 174, 229
erfolgreich 22, 39
Erinnerung 67
erkälten 41
erklären 6
Erleuchtung 141
ermutigen 74
erröten 42
erschöpft 20
Erstarrung 54
Erwartung 8, 10
erwischen 41
Esel 177
Espenlaub 137, 197
essen 73
Eule 39
Exempel 149
Exzentriker 182

Fach 197
fachsimpeln 199, 218
Faden 108, 146, 154, 179, 222
Fährte 165
Fall 16, 36, 37, 40, 55
Falle 136
fallen 115
Fantasie 204
Farbe 48
Fass 135, 211
Fassung 180
Fauna 87
Faust 20, 117
Fäustchen 135
Feder 172
federleicht 15
Fee 79
Fehler 29, 80, 202, 208
Feierabend 38, 47
Feigling 200
Feindschaft 18
Feld 103
fertig 10
festnageln 158
Fettnäpfchen 69, 89
Feuer 85, 164, 165, 175
Feuerprobe 6

finden 84
Finger 29, 84, 85, 97, 108, 130, 141, 155, 202, 227
Firlefanz 91
Fisch 86
fischen 234
fix und fertig 17
fixe Idee 22
Flamme 35, 164, 173
Flasche 53, 60
Flausen 120, 180
Fleisch 55, 207
Fliege 25, 131
Flora 87
fluchen 73
Flucht 190
Flügel 47
flunkern 219
Flur 175
Flut 209
Folgen 36
Fortschritt 199
Frage 22, 138, 182, 201, 231
frech 12
Frechheit 43, 159, 163
Fregatte 68, 131
Freiheit 25, 217
fressen 120
Freude 20
Freund 79, 85, 91, 113
Freundlichkeit 131, 205
Frieden 143, 150
Frucht 90, 92
Früchte 20
Fuchs 123
Fuchtel 223
Führung 112, 186
fünf vor zwölf 17
Fuß 97, 134, 144, 169, 180, 187, 197, 198
Fußstapfen 88

Gang 122, 215
Gängelband 212
Ganovenehre 117
Gänsehaut 87, 97
ganz und gar 29
Gardinenpredigt 55
Gas 210
Gasse 125
Gaul 85, 97
Gedächtnis 38
Gedanke 47, 61, 147, 155
Geduld 17, 213, 226
Gefahr 90, 109, 188
Gefallen 82
gefasst sein/machen 6, 31
Gefecht 113, 180
gefeuert 44
Gefühl 30, 82, 119, 186
Gegenseitigkeit 183
geheim 18, 58
Geheimnis 99, 111, 139, 206
gehupft wie gesprungen 33
Geist 97, 99, 138, 198, 207
geistesabwesend 81, 111, 122
Geistlicher 151
gelassen 51
gelb 104
Geld 47, 72, 76, 131, 143, 156, 172, 173, 193, 206, 210, 223
Geldgier 147
Gelegenheit 8
gemeinsam 228
Gemeinwohl 50
Generalprobe 68
Gerede 204
gerissen 51
Geschäft 35, 46, 198
Geschichte 207
Geschmack 113, 212
geschniegelt 206
Geschwätz 45
geschwätzig 43
Gesellschaft 11, 130
Gesicht 21, 45, 78, 83, 92, 166, 179, 193, 207, 226, 237
Gespräch 35, 212
Geständnis 219
gestern 30, 161
gesund 106, 229
Getümmel 75

gewagt 79
Gewähr 238
Gewalt 7, 24, 34
Gewerbe 165
Gewinn 166
gewinnen 107
gewisses Etwas 112
Gewissen 45, 231
Gewohnheit 90, 106, 150
Gewohnheitstier 219
Gipfel 212
Glanzleistung 54
Glanzstück 170
Glas 182
glasklar 55
Glaube 125
gleich 11, 142
Gleichgewicht 223
gleichgültig 39
Gleis 191
Glotze 31
Glück 10, 23, 42, 62, 90, 115, 124, 148, 202, 221
glücklich 59
Glücksfall 212
Glücksklee 91
Glückstopf 148
Gold 137
golden 102, 207
Goldmine 102
Gott 47, 102, 151, 172, 175, 192, 204, 220
Gottesgeschenk 97
Grab 89
Gras 25, 34, 70, 132
Grenze 67, 202, 210
Griff 94
griffbereit 16
Grimasse 78, 149
Großen und Ganzen 36
Größenwahn 62
größenwahnsinnig 24
Grube 63
grün 26, 38, 106, 147, 235
Gründervater 91
Grundzüge 19
Gunst 82, 198
Gürtel 223
Gürtellinie 115
gut stehen 22
Gute 76

Haar 16, 73, 74, 81, 106, 216, 219
Haarspaltereien 106
Hacken 46
Hahn 117
Hals 74, 112, 165, 200, 223
Halt 108
Hamsterkäufe 136
Hand 39, 40, 48, 73, 74, 84, 85, 98, 104, 107, 110, 113, 118, 136, 138, 151, 158, 166, 183, 187, 197, 201, 206, 216, 218, 228, 233
handeln 7
Handumdrehen 123
Hansdampf 125
Hase 40, 123, 203, 237
Haus 36, 58, 149
Häuschen 18, 20
Haut 19, 72, 88, 121, 193, 199, 202
Hehl 29
Heidenangst 193
Heim 113
Heimweg 151
heimzahlen 75
heiraten 152
heiter 12
helfen 166
Hemd 146
herabsehen 145
herausrücken 49, 52
Herd 113
Hering 169
Herr 102, 125
herumlungern 108
herumnörgeln 129
Herumtoben 118
herunterspielen 150
Herz 19, 30, 66, 105, 111, 113, 144, 181, 196, 217

Heuhaufen 159
Hilfe 79
Himmel 132, 142, 157, 165, 178, 197
Himmelstür 172
hineingeraten 29
hin und her 18
hinauslaufen 29
hinauswerfen 130
Hindernis 223
hineinziehen 67
hinschmeißen 44
Hintergrund 18, 22
Hinterhand 202
hinterherjagen 8
Hintern 130
Hinweis 115
Hinz und Kunz 11
hinzuziehen 33
Hirngespinst 83
hochnäsig 111
Hochtouren 26
Hochzeit 109
Hof machen 57
Hoffnung 34, 58, 125, 164
Hoffnungsschimmer 99, 185
Höhe 229
hohes Tier 24
Hölle 24, 62, 157
Holz 213, 225
Holzweg 20, 210, 216, 225
Honig 35, 134
Honigkuchenpferd 104
Honigschlecken 173
hören 12
Hören 212
Horn 205, 216
Hose 127, 201, 234
Huhn 66, 76
Hühnchen 29, 110
Hund 20, 66, 102, 133, 139, 147, 187, 196, 216
hundeelend 15
Hundeleben 66, 136
Hunger 119
Hut 105, 164, 184, 217

Idee 173
im Allgemeinen 36 181, 196, 217
im Geheimen 22
im Nu 17, 122
im übrigen 14
immer 8, 16
in flagranti 41
Innera 226
irren 75, 117
Irrenanstalt 135
Irrtum 225
interessieren 31

Jacke 201
Jahr 11, 81, 240
Jubeljahre 29, 165
jucken 121
Jugendjahre 192
Junggeselle 50
Junggesellenabschied 207

Kaff 166
Kaiser 69
kalt 15
kaltblütig 27, 48, 122
Kamel 211
Kante 180, 184, 192
Kapital 40
Karriere 9, 95
Karte 136, 200
Kartenhaus 118
Kartenverkauf 31
Kartoffeln 44
Kasse 40, 199
Kater 106
Katerstimmung 156
katzbuckeln 31
Katze 36, 40, 67, 80, 139, 142, 173
Katzensprung 210
käuflich 76
Kauz 164
kehren 118, 226
Kehrseite 167
Keil 68
Keim 160
keineswegs 6

Keller 201
Kerl 61
Kern 180
kerngesund 14
kerzengerade 211
Kelle 41, 233
Kettenreaktion 132
Kieker 67
Kind 19, 26, 165 176, 200, 206
Kinderkram 131
kinderleicht 14
Kinderspiel 44
Kindheit 151
Kino 201
Klappe 36, 125, 131
klar 68
klären 9
klar Schiff 45
Klartext 143, 175
Klasse 25
Klatsch 146, 170
Kleider 84
Kleidung 23
Kleingedruckte 203
Kleinigkeit 182, 225
Kleinkram 26, 163
kleinkriegen 65
Kleinvieh 151
Klemme 24, 62, 116, 117, 223
Klotz 154
klug 110, 112
Klugscheißer 46, 203
knallhart 15
Kneifzange 120
Kneipentour 179
Knie 191
Knochen 202
Knüppel 180, 206, 207
Koch 119
Kohle 109, 184
kommen 49
Kompetenz 100
Kompliment 50, 138
Kompromiss 20, 107, 212
konfrontiert 78
konfus 122
König 55
Kontakt 130
Kontrolle 95, 107
Kopf 19, 22, 34, 43, 108, 110, 112, 115, 120, 126, 130, 140, 158, 159, 165, 169, 173, 174, 180, 184, 188, 194, 196, 210, 226
Korn 103
Krach 232
Kraft 206, 220, 228
Kraftausdruck 212
Kragen 37, 159, 188
krähen 117
Kram 30
krank machen 9
kränken 119
Krankheit 55
Krieg 116
Kriegsbeil 35, 110
Kriegsfuß 57, 163, 233
Krokodilstränen 54
Krone 181, 198
Kropf 159
Kübel 184
Küche 118
Kuchen 7
Kuckucksei 55
Kuh 192
Kumpel 30
Kurs 42
kurzfristig 16

lächeln 193
lachen 135
Lachen 35, 116, 135, 200
Lackaffe 86
Laden 200
Ladenschluss 8
Lage 19
Landei 52
lang 16
Länge 67, 207
Langohr 177
langweilen 61
Last 21, 121

Laster 62
lästern 25
Latein 237
Lauer 232
Lauf 52
Laufbahn 43
Laufende 147
Lauffeuer 207
Laufpass 97, 223
Laune 21, 26, 119, 215, 217
laut 6
Leben 53, 114, 137, 144, 196, 226
lebendig 9, 35
Lebensabend 74
Lebensunterhalt 31, 72
Lebenswandel 42
Leder 137
Lehre 66, 177
Leib 129
Leiche 61, 139, 168, 201
Leid 66
leise 32
Leviten 219
Licht 99, 141, 179, 198, 222
Liebe 147, 148
Liebesmüh' 27
Lippen 108, 140
Liste 152
Loch 68, 135
Löffel 30, 131, 159
Lohn 232
Lorbeeren 136, 187, 209
Los 125
Löwenanteil 143
Luft 46, 115, 230
Luftschlösser 34
Lüge 140, 169
Lügengeschichte 47, 79
Lumpenhändler 184
Lunte 203
Lust 111
Luxusleben 103

Macht 154
Mächtige 24
mahlen 85
Mahlzeit 207
Mammon 84
Mann 151
Märchen 165
Märchenprinz 157
Mark 196
Markt 51
Maßen 24
Maus 174
Medaille 47, 167
meiden 17
meinetwegen 10
Meinung 9, 18, 22, 30, 42, 52, 65, 206, 231
Meister 153, 177
Melodie 172
Menschenverstand 50, 118
Miene 150
Milch 134
Mimose 200
Missverständnisse 45
Mist 151, 154
Mitleid 174
mitleidig 12
mitmachen 12
mitmischen 44, 111
mittendrin 19, 23
Möglichkeiten 6, 17
Moment 13, 20, 107
Mond 152
Mördergrube 113
Mordsspaß 111
Morgenstund' 25
Mücke 150, 211
Mühe 18, 29, 36, 131, 137, 156, 169, 225, 234
Mumm 111
Mund 48, 116, 127, 153, 157, 193, 199, 200, 207, 224, 234
mündlich 37
Münze 47, 78, 98, 192, 218
Murmeltier 202
Musik 172
Muskel 87
Mut 29, 70, 113, 146, 194, 200

Muttersöhnchen 156
mysteriös 46

nachdenken 39
Nachsicht 11
Nächste 43
Nacht 34, 41, 156, 160, 202, 228, 236
Nachteil 17
Nacken 32
nackt 25
Nadel 159
Nagel 115, 158, 180
nagen 73
Naivling 18
Name 38, 150, 176, 206, 228
Narr 88, 89
Naschkatze 215
Nase 27, 79, 88, 161, 176, 189
natürlich 52
Nebel 156
Neid 104
Neige 199
Nerv 97, 159, 169
nerven 112
Nervenbündel 19
nervös 54, 73
Nest 90, 121
neu 32
Neuanfang 35
Neugier 55
Nickerchen 40, 90
Niederlage 78
Niere 181
Niete 67, 134
Not 114, 158, 193, 196, 202, 231, 233
Notgroschen 136
notieren 127
Nu 17
Nummer 17, 192
Nuss 109, 162
Nutzen 156

Oberfläche 184
Oberhand 236
Ochse 69
offensichtlich 13, 15
ohnmächtig 50
Ohr 10, 20, 47, 71, 73, 77, 101, 106, 112, 115, 138, 174, 178, 188, 195, 232, 235
Öl 164
Ölgötzen 69
Opium 167
Ordnung 10, 45, 80, 187, 196, 198, 205
Ort 91, 113, 114

Paar 109
Pack 194
Palme 68
Pandora 167
Panik 20, 207
Papiertiger 169
Papst 156
Paradies 109, 197
Partei 170, 200
Party 31
Patsche 173, 205
Peanuts 43
Pech 15, 67, 147, 148, 221
Pechsträhne 171
Pechtag 184
pedantisch 216
Pest 210
Peter 171
Pfeffer 203
pfeifen 135
Pferd 40, 118, 181, 237
Pflicht 12, 31, 62, 65
Pflichtbesuch 70
Pille 26, 98
Pionierarbeit 26
Plage 162
Plan 110, 229
Platz 174
pleite sein 20, 33
Pornofilm 28
Porzellanladen 142
präzise 15
Preis 16, 43, 51
Pro 178

Probe 69, 220, 226
probieren 178
Problem 54, 124
Prophet 157, 178
Prozess 238
Prüfung 181
Prügel 216
Punkt 176, 205
Pyrrhussieg 181

Quatsch 10
Quelle 92, 118
Quere 54, 230
quietschfidel 14

Rache 187
rächen 17
Rad 163
Rädchen 47
Radieschen 180
rastlos 16
Ratte 185
Räuber 51, 62
Räuberhöhle 21
Rechnung 70, 118, 182, 194, 225
Recht 128, 154, 187
rechtfertigen 12
Rede 111, 218
reden 116
Regel 14, 30, 53, 150
Regen 76, 92, 127, 168
Regenwetter 160
regnen 113, 184
reichlich 19
Reichweite 13
Reihe 210
Reim 181
Reinfall 57, 152
reinknien 18
reinlegen 64
reizen 18
Renner 24
Reserve 124
Reue 22
Richtung 42
Riemen 97
Risiko 42
Rockzipfel 156
Rolle 163
Rosenpfad 178
Ross 118
rot 48
Ruck 104
Rücken 18, 22, 199, 226
Rückschlag 29, 60, 196
Rückzieher 44
Rückzug 21
Ruf 27, 45, 47, 96, 163
Rufweite 106
Ruhe 14, 18, 72, 117, 136, 138, 220, 224
Ruhm 80
Ruhmeshalle 107
ruinieren 237

Sache 175
Sack 143, 173
Sackgasse 26
Saft 127
Samthandschuh 99, 108, 230
Sand 70, 110, 194, 238
Sarg 158
Säugling 18
Säule 174
schäbig 66
Schachtel 164
Schaf 26
Schafspelz 198
Schälchen 52, 82
schämen 197
Schärfe 218
Schatten 175, 180, 197, 198, 214
Schatzkammer 9
Scheck 40
Schein 13
Scheunendrescher 73
Schicksal 81, 194, 220
schief gehen 10
Schiff 185
Schilde 229
Schippe 187, 217
Schlaf 55, 81, 201

schlafen 60
Schlag 16, 163, 166, 201, 208
schlagen 49
schlagfertig 182
Schlamassel 84, 85
schlau 15
schlicht 179
schließlich 8
Schlips 224
Schlot 203
Schmeichelei 204
Schmetterlinge 35
schmieden 124
schmieren 103
Schmiergeld 164
Schmutz 64
Schnäppchen 20
Schnecke 32, 110, 127
schneeweiß 15
Schnitzer 32
schnorren 34
Schnorrer 91
schnüffeln 161
Schnürchen 46, 101
Schock 86, 199
schön 42
Schönheit 22, 185
Schoß 201
Schrank 111
Schranken 129
Schraube 111, 146
Schrei 11, 184
Schritt 130, 217
Schuh 181, 199
Schuld 38, 136, 181, 189, 227
Schulter 48, 97, 48
Schürzenzipfel 156
Schuss 233
Schuster 47
Schutz 228
schützen 53
Schutzengel 105
schwach 18
Schwäche 207
Schwachpunkt 27
schwachsinnig 157
Schwachstelle 44
Schwalbe 166
Schwamm 139
Schwanz 216, 236
schwänzen 117
schwärmen 129
schwarz 26, 29, 122, 218, 232
Schwarze 117
schwarzes Schaf 26
Schwätzchen 43
Schweigen 177
Schwein 143
Schweiß 37
schwer nehmen 39
schwerhörig 109
Schwert 155, 172
Schwierigkeit 13, 15, 51, 54, 109, 122, 194, 223, 229, 234
schwimmen 62
Schwindel 50
Seele 43, 96, 131
Seemannsgarn 86, 207
Segel 206, 237
Sehen 212
Sekunde 22, 66
selbstverständlich 14
Seligkeit 209
Semmel 38, 118
Sensationspresse 105
Seufzer 32
Show 209
sich drücken 31, 64
sicher 10, 23, 41, 192
Sicherheit 15
sicherlich 15
Sieg 39, 48
Siegel 46
Silber 137
Sinn 48, 75, 111, 161, 214, 235, 237
Sinneswandel 42
Sippe 15
sofort 17
Sohn 142, 178
Sommer 166
Sonne 41
sonnenklar 15

Sonntagsstaat 123
Sorge 136, 213
Spanner 172
sparen 56
Spaß 5, 57, 90, 111, 131, 135, 217
Spatz 25, 73, 107
Spiel 31, 33, 94, 110, 150, 175, 208
spielen 175
Spielregel 94
Spielverderber 26, 235
Spieß 226
spindeldürr 19
Sprache 40, 146, 206
Sprung 126, 176
Spur 53, 130, 159, 225
spüren 82
Stadt 169
Standpauke 68
Standpunkt 108, 198
Staub 131, 193
Steckenpferd 187
Stegreif 107
Stein 13, 19
Steinwurf 210
Stempel 208
sterben 54
Stern 15, 55, 185
Stich 18, 138, 139, 232
Stiefel 140
Stier 216
stillschweigend 186
Stimme 184, 231
Stimmung 216
stinkfaul 29
stinksauer 117
Stirn 92, 77, 78, 132
stockbesoffen 69
stockblind 14
stocktaub 60
Stolperstein 213
Stolz 35, 214
Strafe 232
Stränge 130
Straße 151
Streber 71
Strecke 33, 119
Streich 177
Streik 123
Streit 111
streiten 182, 238
Streitfrage 13
Strich 8, 11, 100, 154, 182, 192
Strick 121
Strippe 28
Strohfeuer 86
Strohhalm 41, 212
Stubenarrest 104
Stubenhocker 116
Stück 25, 58, 196, 219
Stuhl 201
Sturm 211
Sande 232
Sündenbock 79
Sündenpfuhl 62
Suppe 88
Süßes 111
Szene 238

Tacheles 96
Tag 25, 26, 44, 46, 52, 59, 67, 34, 41, 122, 166
Tagedieb 178
Tagesanbruch 16
Tageslicht 33, 141
Taktik 43
Tal 230
tanzen 210
Tasche 23, 64, 132, 175, 207
Tasse 23, 111
Tat 7, 102, 156, 177
Tatendrang 21
Tatsachen 204
tatsächlich 7
taub 60, 80, 226
Taube 107
Teamgeist 219
Telefonhörer 109
Tellerrand 39
Tellerwäscher 91
teuer 51
Teufel 22, 57, 69, 81, 114, 118, 159, 206

Teufelskreis 122, 231
Theater 7, 150
Tiefe 229
Tiefgang 44
Tiefpunkt 115
Tiefschlaf 134
Tinte 154
tipptopp 206
Tisch 45, 136, 214
Toast 114
Tobak 212
Tod 16, 41, 127, 193
Todeskuss 132
Todesstoß 205
todmüde 60
Todsünde 197
Ton 38, 42, 161, 226
Torheit 89
tot 59
töten 65
Toter 184, 232
Träne 35, 188, 198
Tratsch 146
Traufe 127, 168
Traum 57
traurig 73
Treiben 119
Treue 175
Tricks 19
Tritt 180
Trockene 234
trödeln 134
Tropfen 135, 211
tropfen 69
Trost 11, 48, 126, 159
Trottel 7
trotzdem 10, 11
Trübe 234
Trumpfkarte 20
Tuch 186
Tugend 170, 171, 184, 231
Tunichtgut 103
Tür 34, 46, 118, 167
turteln 25
typisch 10, 11

übel 12
Übel 62, 139, 186
überall 11
überarbeiten 39
übereinstimmen 12
überlegen 23
Überlegung 195, 222
überraschen 21
Überraschung 30, 214, 235
überschätzen 5
überschlagen 80
übertreffen 23
übertreiben 136
übertrieben 81
überzeugen 39, 40
Uhr 46, 184, 202
Uhrwerk 15
Umschweife 211
Umweg 189
unerfahren 44
unerträglich 24
Unfug 144
ungewiss 9
Ungewissen 130
unglaublich 38
Unglück 124, 177, 184
unhöflich 18
Unkenntnis 129
Unkraut 121
unordentlich 13
Unruhe 40
Unschuld 45, 233
Unsinn 120, 213
unter „ferner liefen“ 12
unterbrechen 56
Unterstützung 36, 83
Untersuchung 21
unterwürfig 39
unvernünftig 25
unverschämt 14
unverständlich 14
unvorstellbar 24
Urteil 171

Vater 113, 142
verabscheuen 110

verabschieden 24
Verantwortung 12, 18, 26, 38, 198, 217
verantwortungsbewusst 7
Verbindung 224
Verbot 210
verbünden 121
Verdacht 5
Verderben 51
verdrängen 74
Verfassung 15, 50, 122
verflixt 58
Verfügung 13
vergeben 90
vergewissern 41
Vergleich 8
vergöttern 222
Verhältnis 24, 144
verkommen 184
verlassen 114
Verlegenheit147, 181
verletzen 56
verlieben 79
verloren gehen 7
Verlust 166
vernachlässigbar 43
vernachlässigen 139
Vernunft 33, 231
verpetzen 219
verraten 21, 28, 204
verrotten 209
verrückt 15, 68, 112, 148, 149, 162
Verrücktheit 118
verschonen 139
Versenkung 201
Verstand 230
Versuch 226
Versuchskaninchen 105
Vertrauen 113, 122
Vertrautheit 80
verunglücken 6
verursachen 33
verzählen 52
verzaubern 234
Verzweiflung 68
Vogel 20, 25, 88, 142, 201
Volldampf 10
vollfressen 28
volljährig 9
volltrunken 27
vorbeikommen 68
vorbeischauen 38, 68
vorbeugen 178
Vorbild 105
vorlesen 185
Vorliebe 143
Vorschein 33
Vorsicht 64
Vorstellung 120
Vorteil 8, 121, 226, 231

Wagen 163
Wahl 44
Wahnsinn 231
wahnsinnig 68
Wahrheit 49, 71, 141, 155
Wald 161
Wand 18, 46, 232
Wandervogel 25
Wange 188
wappnen 13
wann 115
warnen 39
warten 51
waschen 173
Wasser 39, 58, 61, 80, 104, 112, 130, 147, 157, 164, 210, 214, 225, 234, 238
Wässerchen 35
Wasserglas 211
Wechselgeld 42
Wechseljahre 42
Weg 26, 136, 137, 150, 153, 172, 203, 223, 225, 234, 237
wegkommen 23
Wehwehchen 6
weinen 55, 135
weise 15
Weisheit 16
weiterwursteln 126
Wellen 41
Welt 20, 51, 124, 135, 141, 164

Wenn und Aber 35
wenig 8
Werbebranche 114
Wert 176, 211
Wespennest 117
Wetter 234
Wettkampf 190
Wettlauf 8, 224
wichtig 40
Widerspruch 11
Widerstand 8, 208
wiederkäuen 43
Wiege 91
Wildnis 119
Wille 124, 234, 236, 237
willkommen 30
wimmeln 10
Wimper 20, 226
Wind 28, 47, 96, 206. 237
Wink 115
Winkel 161
Wirt 118
Wissen 8, 9, 23
Witz 53
Witzfigur 83
Woche 59
Wogen 177
Wolf 123, 144, 198
Wolke 47
Wort 18, 32, 84, 96, 120, 135, 156, 157, 180, 217, 224, 235, 238, 239
Wörtchen 111
Wunde 140
Wunder 238
wunderbar 84
Würgen 202
Wurzel 188, 212, 219
Wut 27, 28, 87, 219
Wutanfall 110
wütend 15

zäh 15
Zahl 185
zählen 52
Zahn 13, 19, 46, 104, 210
Zähneknirschen 100
Zankapfel 13, 30
zanken 80
Zauber 32
Zaunpfahl 115
Zeche 197
Zeile 23, 185
Zeit 5, 9, 10, 52, 59, 66, 85, 114, 115, 122, 131, 139, 154, 171, 189, 224, 233
Zeitdruck 224
Zeitvertreib 187
zerronnen 72
Zeter 28
Zeug 56
Ziel 168, 185, 201
ziellos 115
zieren 9
zischen 33
Zivilcourage 111
Zorn 78
zu Hause 72
Zuckerbrot 39
Zufall 138
zufällig 6, 36, 42
Zufallsbekanntschaft 42
Zufriedenheit 226
Zug 2, 155
Zügel 186
Zugeständnis 176
Zukunft 101, 145
zum Besten halten 94
zumuten 25
Zunge 32, 46, 111, 146, 224
Zünglein 19
zusammenreißen 7
zu sprechen 30
Zustimmung 36
zwanglos 72
Zwangsvorstellung 86
Zweck 12, 62, 196, 230,
zwei 219, 227
Zweifel 23, 160
Zwietracht 205
zwölf 74
zynisch 125